TM

References for the Rest of Us!®

BESTSELLING BOOK SERIES

Do you find that traditional reference books are overloaded with technical details and advice you'll never use? Do you postpone important life decisions because you just don't want to deal with them? Then our *For Dummies®* business and general reference book series is for you.

For Dummies business and general reference books are written for those frustrated and hard-working souls who know they aren't dumb, but find that the myriad of personal and business issues and the accompanying horror stories make them feel helpless. *For Dummies* books use a lighthearted approach, a down-to-earth style, and even cartoons and humorous icons to dispel fears and build confidence. Lighthearted but not lightweight, these books are perfect survival guides to solve your everyday personal and business problems.

Already, millions of satisfied readers agree. They have made For Dummies the #1 introductory level computer book series and a best-selling business book series. They have written asking for more. So, if you're looking for the best and easiest way to learn about business and other general reference topics, look to For Dummies to give you a helping hand.

Wiley Publishing, Inc.

5/09

Boxers

FOR

DUMMIES®

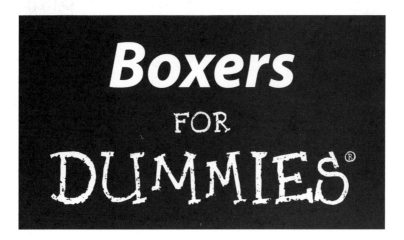

Boxers FOR DUMMIES®

by Richard Beauchamp

WILEY

Wiley Publishing, Inc.

Boxers For Dummies®

Published by
Wiley Publishing, Inc.
111 River Street
Hoboken, NJ 07030
www.wiley.com

Copyright © 2000 by Wiley Publishing, Inc., Indianapolis, Indiana

Published by Wiley Publishing, Inc., Indianapolis, Indiana

Published simultaneously in Canada

For general information on our other products and services or to obtain technical support, please contact our Customer Care Department within the U.S. at 877-762-2974, outside the U.S. at 317-572-3993, or fax 317-572-4002.

Wiley also publishes its books in a variety of electronic formats. Some content that appears in print may not be available in electronic books.

Library of Congress Cataloging-in-Publication Data:

Library of Congress Control Number: 00-106305

ISBN 10: 0-7645-5285-6

ISBN 13: 978-0-7645-5285-4

Manufactured in the United States of America

15 14

1B/RQ/QS/QY/IN

About the Author

So, who made **Rick Beauchamp** the know-all Dog Tsar? In a word (well, two words), no one. Nor is anything in this book divinely inspired. According to Rick, any and all useful information in *Boxers For Dummies* is here because it was passed down to him by his mentors in purebred dogs or through good old-fashioned trial and error.

Over the past half century, Rick has experienced and enjoyed nearly every facet of purebred dogs — breeding, exhibiting, professional handling, publishing, writing, lecturing, and judging. He has had the good fortune to have bred over 100 champions and noted dog show winners under his Beau Monde kennel prefix in a number of different breeds, including his special pals — Boxers.

Rick's judging assignments have taken him to practically every major dog-showing country in the world, and this has given him the opportunity to judge Boxers in most every instance. He now judges for the American Kennel Club and the United Kennel Club in the United States.

About Howell Book House
Committed to the Human/Companion Animal Bond

Thank you for choosing a book brought to you by the pet experts at Howell Book House, a division of Wiley Publishing, Inc. And welcome to the family of pet owners who've put their trust in Howell books for nearly 40 years!

Pet ownership is about relationships — the bonds people form with their dogs, cats, horses, birds, fish, small mammals, reptiles, and other animals. Howell Book House/Wiley understands that these are some of the most important relationships in life, and that it's vital to nurture them through enjoyment and education. The happiest pet owners are those who know they're taking the best care of their pets — and with Howell books owners have this satisfaction. They're happy, educated owners, and as a result, they have happy pets, and that enriches the bond they share.

Howell Book House was established in 1961 by Mr. Elsworth S. Howell, an active and proactive dog fancier who showed English Setters and judged at the prestigious Westminster Kennel Club show in New York. Mr. Howell based his publishing program on strength of content, and his passion for books written by experienced and knowledgeable owners defined Howell Book House and has remained true over the years. Howell's reputation as the premier pet book publisher is supported by the distinction of having won more awards from the Dog Writers Association of America than any other publisher. Howell Book House/Wiley has over 400 titles in publication, including such classics as The American Kennel Club's *Complete Dog Book,* the *Dog Owner's Home Veterinary Handbook, Blessed Are the Brood Mares,* and *Mother Knows Best: The Natural Way to Train Your Dog.*

When you need answers to questions you have about any aspect of raising or training your companion animals, trust that Howell Book House/Wiley has the answers. We welcome your comments and suggestions, and we look forward to helping you maximize your relationships with your pets throughout the years.

The Howell Book House Staff

Publisher

Howell Book House/Wiley Publishing, Inc.

Author's Acknowledgments

Boxers For Dummies would have remained an idea floating around in my head rather than the reality it has become had it not been for my Project Editor Elizabeth Kuball and all the other great people at Wiley. They patiently and effectively helped me transform years of accumulated knowledge and experience into what I hope will be your ready reference for a lifetime of being owned by a Boxer.

Thanks are also most certainly due to the many mentors I have had in purebred dogs through the years. Their love and understanding of all dogs guided me along the path I have had to a rich and rewarding life.

Most of all a special thank you to Ginger, who was our family's first Boxer and the dog who inspired a lifetime of admiration for the breed on my part.

Publisher's Acknowledgments

Acknowledgments

We're proud of this book; please send us your comments through our Online Registration Form located at www.dummies.com/register.

Some of the people who helped bring this book to market include the following:

Acquisitions, Editorial, and Media Development

Project Editor: Elizabeth Netedu Kuball

Acquisitions Editor: Scott Prentzas

Technical Editor: William Truesdale, D.V.M.

Editorial Manager: Pamela Mourouzis

Editorial Assistant: Carol Strickland

Cover Photo: © Tracy Hendrickson

Composition

Project Coordinator: Nancee Reeves

Layout and Graphics: Jason Guy, Stephanie D. Jumper, Tracy K. Oliver, Brian Torwelle, Erin Zeltner

Proofreaders: Corey Bowen, Vickie Broyles, Betty Kish, Susan Moritz, Toni Settle

Indexer: Rebecca R. Plunkett

Publishing and Editorial for Consumer Dummies

Diane Graves Steele, Vice President and Publisher, Consumer Dummies

Joyce Pepple, Acquisitions Director, Consumer Dummies

Kristin A. Cocks, Product Development Director, Consumer Dummies

Michael Spring, Vice President and Publisher, Travel

Brice Gosnell, Associate Publisher, Travel

Suzanne Jannetta, Editorial Director, Travel

Publishing for Technology Dummies

Richard Swadley, Vice President and Executive Group Publisher

Andy Cummings, Vice President and Publisher

Composition Services

Gerry Fahey, Vice President of Production Services

Debbie Stailey, Director of Composition Services

Contents at a Glance

Cartoons at a Glance

By Rich Tennant

page 7

page 109

page 63

page 169

page 31

Fax: 978-546-7747
E-mail: richtennant@the5thwave.com
World Wide Web: www.the5thwave.com

Table of Contents

Introduction

. . . .

*O*ne thing we know for sure is that our next dog will never. . . ." If I've heard those words once, I've heard them a million times. And I have to include myself in making that same adamant declaration.

Quite frankly, I wish I had known what I know now when I got my first dog. When I've thought back on the trials and tribulations I faced with my first Boxer and compare them to the relative ease with which subsequent dogs adapted to my lifestyle, it made me think I should write a book. So I have!

Boxers For Dummies can introduce new or prospective owners to the ins and outs of being owned by a Boxer. But it also reminds all of us — veteran or novice — of the Boxer's vast storehouse of unique qualities, qualities that exist in a raw and undeveloped state and that require our attention before they can develop to their greatest potential.

Boxers: The Good, the Bad, and the Ugly

In these pages, you'll be introduced to all the good, the bad, and the ugly that surrounds the breed. Too many books written about purebred dogs do nothing but try to convince you that the breed is not only flawless but suitable for every household in America (or anywhere else in the world for that matter). I seldom find this to be true of any breed, and I know this doesn't describe the Boxer. So you won't find me twisting your arm and trying to convince you that a Boxer's right for you. In fact, if anything, I'm as honest as possible. That way, if you're still eager to get one of these wonderful dogs, you'll be prepared for any negatives and able to handle them well.

Boxers have to be one of the smartest, most trainable breeds I have ever known. Not only is the Boxer capable of learning just about everything any other breed can master, the Boxer also has the energy, the strength, and the enthusiasm to carry it all off with style! He's funny and good natured, and I have yet to meet a Boxer who was mean.

Along with all those perfect dog qualities I've attributed to the Boxer, there are a few drawbacks. A young Boxer can find more things to get into than an army of ants let loose in the pantry. Boxers are nosy and investigative and they have the determination and athleticism to follow any clue they find to its logical (or illogical) conclusion! You get all of these traits right along with all the angelic qualities. However, time and experience make us all masters at training a dog, and I pass along lots of useful tips throughout this book.

The Boxer whose owner has neglected training is nothing but a big nuisance. Although a Boxer is rarely a fighter, his extremely extroverted personality can drive the neighbors' cats, dogs, and kids up a tree — literally and figuratively. That comic personality can get too far over the top as well. An untrained Boxer acting on his own volition can be far from a laughing matter.

So Who Am I?

Nothing in this book came by way of divine inspiration. Everything in *Boxers For Dummies* is the result of my own years of trial and error or through the kind intervention of my many mentors through the years.

My interest in purebred dogs goes back as far as I can remember and has led me through practically every facet of these wonderful animals: breeding, exhibiting, professional handling, publishing, writing, and judging. All that experience has also assisted me in presenting lectures to dog fanciers around the world.

For over 30 years, I owned and published *Kennel Review Magazine,* and doing so associated me with some of the most learned dog men and women the world over. As a breeder/exhibitor, using the Beau Monde kennel prefix, I have bred nearly 100 American Kennel Club champions in a number of different breeds, including Boxers.

My judging assignments have taken me to practically every major dog showing country in the world, which has given me the opportunity to judge Boxers in almost every instance. I now judge for both the American Kennel Club and the United Kennel Club here in the United States.

Most importantly, of course, I love Boxers, and I've lived with them for years. The tips and suggestions you'll find in these pages aren't only for those who are interested in showing their dogs. Even if your Boxer's idea of competition is seeing how fast he can get to his food dish, this book is for you.

How This Book Is Organized

Boxers For Dummies is divided into five parts. If you're just starting to think about getting a Boxer, try starting out with Chapter 1. If you already own a Boxer and have a specific question or problem, dive into the chapter that best suits your needs right now.

Part I: Getting to Know Boxers

In this part, you'll get a feel for Boxers as a breed. Then you'll set about to determine whether a Boxer is right for you. Everyone's needs and personalities are different, and before you head out to the nearest breeder to find a Boxer pup, you owe it to yourself and the dog you may bring home to do some serious soul-searching.

Part II: Finding Your Soul Mate

The chapters in this part are geared toward helping you figure out what you actually want in a Boxer. You may be sure a Boxer's right for you. But Boxers vary just like people do. So knowing your lifestyle and priorities is just as important at this stage in the game as it is in determining what breed you want.

You also need to know where to look for your new best friend. So I guide you through the process of finding a reputable breeder and tell you which ones to steer clear of altogether.

Finally, you get to the fun stuff: picking out a puppy. Sometimes looking at all the pups in a litter makes you want to bring them *all* home. So in this part I let you know which traits to look for in a puppy, physically and emotionally.

Part III: Living with a Boxer

In this part, you plan ahead so that you have all the toys and tools you'll need before that plump little pup arrives. Here you make sure you have all the supplies and tools you'll need for the homecoming. And you also get tips on introducing your Boxer pup to his new home. Finally, no puppy would be a puppy without the need for training. So you'll figure out which behaviors to start working on with your Boxer from the very first day. And you'll also get tips on which behaviors your dog should know as he grows into adulthood. You even get suggestions for going the extra mile with your dog and going through more formal obedience training with a professional trainer.

Living with a Boxer? Here I make it one of life's greatest joys.

Part IV: Maintaining Your Boxer's Health

Many dog owners accept as fact the stories they've heard for generations, when the stories are, in reality, pure fiction. Knowing what makes your Boxer tick and how to keep that well-functioning clock in perfect order are important if you want your pal to live a long and healthy life. This includes knowing what to feed your dog and how much exercise to give her. In the chapters in this part, you get information on anything and everything that pertains to your Boxer's health.

An ounce of prevention is most definitely worth a pound of cure. So I let you know how to prevent your dog from getting sick by taking care of him along the way.

Accidents and illnesses are not always avoidable, so being fully prepared for these events is always wise. In this part, you'll find instructions for dealing with emergencies involving your dog. And you'll know what chronic health problems sometimes affect Boxers as they age and how best to handle them.

Part V: The Part of Tens

In this part, you get lots of useful information in a small amount of space. Whether you're trying to figure out whether to get a Boxer, or you want to find ways to have fun with the one you already have, there's something in this part for you. I offer some useful tips on traveling with your pet and training him as well. In a time crunch? Turn to this part.

Icons Used in This Book

Icons are those eye-catching little pictures in the margins of this book. They're meant to grab your attention as you flip the pages, and they steer you to specific bits of information you need. Here's a list of the icons in this book and what I use them for:

If you're looking for information on how to do something better, look for the Tip icon.

Whenever something could harm your Boxer, I flag it with this icon.

This icon is the place to turn for information that you can use to impress your friends at the dog park. But you probably don't *need* to know it. If you just want the basics, pass by these paragraphs.

Some pieces of information are so important that they're worth repeating. So when you see this icon, pay attention. Because the information nearby includes things you'll want to remember.

Throughout this book you'll find interesting anecdotes or funny stories about Boxers that are great for a laugh but probably aren't critical to knowing what you need to know. I flag them with this icon.

Occasionally, I toss in products or services that are useful to Boxer owners, and I highlight them with this wagging tail. (In the Boxer's case, maybe it should be just a wagging rear end.)

Part I
Getting to Know Boxers

The 5th Wave   By Rich Tennant

"As Boxers go, he's good at heeling on command and rolling over, but he still drops his left making him vulnerable to an overhand right."

In this part . . .

In this part, I let you know all the basics you need on Boxers as a breed. I also guide you through the process of figuring out whether a Boxer is the right dog for you. If you're just getting started, this is the place to begin.

Chapter 1

What Is a Boxer?

So you're interested in Boxers? Maybe you're thinking about getting one, but you're not quite sure what sets the Boxer apart from other breeds. Or maybe you already have a Boxer, and you're dying to know more about your dog. If you fit either of these descriptions, this is the chapter for you.

In this chapter, you get the lowdown on the history of dogs and the history of Boxers in particular. (Don't worry . . . this is one history lesson you won't snooze through.) I also give you the scoop on the American Kennel Club (AKC) and the standards it sets for the Boxer breed. Plus, I answer that age-old question: Does it matter if my lovable dog fits the breed standard? If you're interested in finding out more information on this wonderful breed, read on.

Canine History 101

As you probably know, every dog breed known to man is a descendant of *Canis Lupus,* otherwise known as the wolf. But have you ever stopped to think about how man domesticated the wolf and helped him evolve into the animals we now know as "man's best friend"?

It all started with a few hungry wolves. . . .

It seems that, thousands of years ago, mankind had a waste-removal problem. (Not much has changed in the past few millennia.) A resolution to the mounting problem of trash turned out to be none other than the wolf, who started to realize that rummaging around the trash heap was a much easier way to find lunch than hunting it down.

Because the wolf spent a good deal of time nearby, waiting to see what was on the menu, the Mesolithic man had the chance to observe — and copy — some of the wolf's survival techniques. The wolf pack's communal style of living was an excellent example of safety in numbers, not to mention team spirit. And the pack lifestyle obviously worked in the pack's favor when it came time to hunt.

Just as the wolf started to see some value in hanging around man, the Mesolithic man started to recognize the value of the wolf. So instead of including wolf meat as part of the clan's diet, they decided to allow some members of the wolf family to camp out nearby, undisturbed.

As the relationship thickened, the better-behaved members of the wolf pack moved right into town. The clan folk undoubtedly began to realize they could select certain descendants of these increasingly friendly wolves to help around the settlement, by doing things like hunting, pulling large objects, and sounding the alarm when marauding neighbors threatened or a mastodon came calling. These qualities were all ones the settlement people began to prize in their wolves. By then, the humans were becoming clever enough to start serving as matchmakers for the wolves — and matching up the right pairs made better, more reliable workers out of the next generation. Man realized that, through selection, they could customize the wolves to suit more specific needs.

And roughly around this time in history, we stop calling the animals *wolves* and start referring to them as *Canis Familiaris,* or, for the non-Latin speaking among us, *dogs.* Particular characteristics were prized and inbreeding practices were used to intensify these desired characteristics. As time passed, these positive physical characteristics and attitudes became more and more obvious, first setting dogs apart from wolves, and then setting dogs apart from one another. These characteristics were recorded and became the forerunners of what we now call *breed standards.*

Some of the earliest breed standards only described what the breed looked like, whereas others offered a word picture of how the dog should relate to man. Each country had dogs for different purposes, and their breed standards reflected this. The Germans and English became especially noted for the many breeds they developed, Germany taking particular pride in the quality of what we refer to today as *working* or *guard dogs.* Of the many such breeds developed in Germany, some became real standouts: German Shepherds, Doberman Pinschers, Rottweilers, and our friend the Boxer caught the attention of dog fanciers everywhere.

The Germans who developed the Boxer wanted a breed that was courageous and protective. Certainly, the Boxer can be both. But I wonder if they had any idea that they were also creating a breed that had a stand-up comic's sense of humor? All we can do today is wonder how that gene for outrageous humor found its way into the Boxer gene pool.

The German standard for the Boxer

Through the years, Germany has developed a reputation for producing many scientific minds. So not at all surprising is the fact that dog fanciers in Germany approached breeding with a very exacting and demanding set of rules and regulations.

In Germany, dog breeding was never a case of taking Topsy down the street to get her hitched up to the neighborhood Lothario. As new breeds were created, German fanciers organized clubs to improve and protect their respective breeds.

If people wanted to breed dogs, they had to join the club dedicated to the breed and abide by the club's rules and regulations.

The first club that really united German Boxer fanciers was the Boxer Klub mit dem Sitz in Munich. In 1902, the organization drew up a standard of perfection that was based upon Flock St. Salvator, an outstanding Boxer of the time. All standards, including that used in America today, have their roots in that 1902 standard.

The Boxer's evolution in Europe

By the time the Romans were attending games in amphitheaters, man had evolved to a level of sophistication that was reflected in many ways. Separate classes of society had developed — so, to put it simply, there were those who did the work and those who sat around and thought up all kinds of work for everyone else to do. One of the ideas thought up by the latter group was a way to further meddle with nature and make more breeds of dogs out of those that already existed.

The noble ladies of Rome had tiny lapdogs, who sat on their laps and kept them company. But "real" men (the ones who didn't eat quiche) had dogs who were large enough and fierce enough to fight lions, tigers, and assorted other wild beasts in the arena. (Certainly an illuminating comment on the heights to which man's capabilities had risen — or fallen, depending on your point of view — from his days back in the caves.)

Only the largest, strongest, and fiercest of the Mastiff-type dogs were ever allowed to fight in the Roman arenas. These brawny beasts were known as the *Mollosus,* and although there were undoubtedly many candidates for the honor of tearing to pieces everything in sight, not all of the dogs qualified. From the same litters that produced the elite arena dogs came the dogs who became guards, protectors, and draft dogs. Until the Middle Ages, these dogs were known as *Alains* or *Alaunts.* In England, these same large and fierce dogs became known as *Bandogs,* because bands, ropes, and chains were used to keep them under control.

Some of the dogs who weren't qualified to fight in the Roman arenas were used in England to assist butchers in controlling the savage bulls that would later be killed and sold, perhaps to be eaten for dinner by one of the town's citizens. Common belief at the time was that the meat of the bulls that had been "worried" by these Bandogs prior to butchering was much more tender and nutritious than the meat that came from those bulls that were immediately slaughtered.

The dogs who assisted the butchers with the bulls were eventually bred to have shorter legs and heavier bodies. This construction served the dogs well in keeping out of the way of the bulls' horns. What was simply a functional animal doing his job was rapidly adapted to salve man's ego: Thus was the sport of *bullbaiting* born. In bullbaiting contests, the dog was supposed to bite the bull on the nose when the tethered bull attempted to impale the dog on its horns. The undershot jaw of the *Bullenbeiser* dog enabled the dog to clamp on to the bull's nose with such a vice-like grip that it was virtually impossible for the bull to dislodge the dog and escape. The dog's heavy body weight and lower center of gravity, combined with his sheer grit and determination, could eventually bring the bull to the ground. And the dog was expected to hold on to the bull with no regard to his own personal injury, until the bull finally fell, dying from blood loss and oxygen deprivation.

As the bullbaiting sport grew, man found that the smaller Bullenbeisers were better at their assigned task in the bullbaiting rings than the giant version of the dog. And with time, the breed was eventually divided into two size categories. The smaller and more useful became known as the *Brabanter,* and the larger dogs became known as *Danzigers.* It is from the Brabanter that most historians believe the Boxer is descended.

The mother of the modern-day Boxer

No history of the Boxer would be complete without mentioning Friederun Stockmann, who almost single-handedly earned the reputation as the mother of the modern-day breed. Frau Stockmann came on the already somewhat popular Boxer scene in 1911 and spent the rest of her life perfecting the breed through her line of Boxers known as the *von Dom bloodline.*

Stockmann's devotion to the breed survived the catastrophic events of two world wars. During those years, Germany was reduced to such extreme economic circumstances that Frau Stockmann was often forced to choose between feeding her beloved Boxers and putting food on her own table.

With the assistance of the Boxer Club in Munich, Frau Stockmann was able to convince the government to use the breed in the war effort. The breed's great speed, intelligence, and agility proved to be such invaluable assets to the German army that Boxers became the pioneer war dogs. The innate bravery and eagerness of the Boxer to serve his master are undoubtedly what helped save the breed from being totally obliterated by Germany's chaotic war years.

Anchors aweigh!: The movement of the Boxer to the New World

The first Boxer registered by the American Kennel Club was Arnulf Grandenz in 1904. Surprisingly, Arnulf was not imported from Germany but was instead an American-bred dog, bred and owned by Max H. Schachner in Downers Grove, Illinois.

In 1914, Herbert H. Lehman, a future Governor of New York, imported Dampf von Dom, a Boxer who had won many prizes at shows in Germany. Dampf duplicated his winning ways in the U.S. by quickly becoming the first American champion for the breed.

Initially, however, the Boxer did not inspire much enthusiasm among American dog fanciers. Not until 1930 did interest in the breed develop, and from that point forward, the popularity of the Boxer began to skyrocket. The American Boxer Club was organized in 1935, signifying the breed's growing popularity. As World War II drew to a close, Americans had more money to spend than many of them knew what to do with. Sports and hobbies like dog breeding and dog showing began to attract interest. And the Boxer benefited from this economic prosperity, as did other breeds. The American Boxer Club held its first independent Specialty Show at the Hotel McAlpin in New York City in January 1944. By 1946, the Boxer ranked fifth among all breeds registered by the AKC in terms of popularity.

In the years immediately following World War II, three American-bred Boxers fanned the flames of popularity for the breed by winning Best In Show at the famed Westminster Kennel Club show in New York. In 1947, Ch. Warlord of Mazelaine was victorious at Westminster, and two years later Ch. Mazelaine's Zazarac Brady repeated the victory for the Boxer breed. Ch. Bang Away of Sirrah Crest was Westminster's Best In Show winner in 1951, and he did not stop there. By the time he retired, Bang Away had acquired over 100 all breed Best In Show wins and maintains that distinction for the breed to this day.

Since those triumphant Boxer years, only one other Boxer has been able to take home Westminster's highest honor. In 1970, Ch. Arriba's Prima Donna, the only female of Westminster's Best In Show Boxer quartet, was chosen Best by Anna Katherine Nicholas.

The AKC top ten breeds

Every year, the AKC keeps track of the number of dogs that are registered in each breed. I consider the most popular breeds to be the most endangered, because they often fall victim to puppy mills and backyard breeders, who have no regard for the welfare of the breed or high breeding standards. Here is the list of the most popular (or most endangered) dogs from 1999:

- Labrador Retrievers (154,897)
- Golden Retrievers (62,652)
- German Shepherds (57,256)
- Dachshunds (50,772)
- Beagles (49,080)
- Poodles (45,852)
- Chihuahuas (42,013)
- Rottweilers (41,776)
- Yorkshire Terriers (40,684)
- Boxers (34,998)

The popularity of the Boxer today

In the late 1940s, the Boxer became so popular that it seemed like everyone who had a backyard larger than a postage stamp found a Boxer to put in it. Although popularity often seems like a good thing to the general public, in the world of dog breeding, more is definitely *not* better. The more popular a breed becomes, the greater the prevalence of puppy mills and backyard breeders, who try to capitalize on the breed's popularity without paying any attention to maintaining the quality and high standards of the breed. Any time puppy mills and backyard breeders do business, nothing positive results. In fact, if anything, they only endanger the breed in question.

In 1999, the American Kennel Club registered 34,998 Boxers, representing a drop of a little over 1,000 registrations from the year before. That number means that the Boxer ranks tenth in popularity among the 148 breeds the AKC actually registers.

Acquiring "Top Ten" status may cast a warm glow in some circles, but in purebred dogs, it sends a cold chill down the spines of concerned breeders. The last thing Boxer breeders want to see is a repetition of what happened to the breed during the exploitative 1940s.

Making Sense of the AKC Breed Standard

Currently, the AKC offers the prospective dog owner 148 breeds to choose from, and upwards of 400 breeds are recognized worldwide. They range from Chihuahuas (one of the tiniest toy breeds, weighing in under 6 pounds) to the giant breeds (which include man-sized Great Danes and Irish Wolfhounds). Almost every breed was developed with a specific purpose in mind. The reasons behind the development of the various breeds may be very different from one another, but you can count on the fact that someone, at some point in time, decided there was something about a specific dog that needed to be preserved and perpetuated.

Dogs have been bred to do everything from sitting on the laps of well-to-do ladies to hunting small game to hauling large loads. The size, shape, and temperament of each breed have all been carefully manipulated by man through many generations to conform to an ideal. To this day, in order for a purebred dog to be a representative of his breed, the dog must have both the look and the attitude typical of that breed.

Understanding breed standards

The presiding kennel club of each country has a registering system for the purebred dogs that are born and bred in their country. The American Kennel Club (AKC) is the recognized authority in the United States. These registering systems issue certificates of legitimacy, which are probably best described as canine birth certificates. The only way a dog can be considered a purebred and be registered is if the dog's father and mother (sire and dam in dog parlance) are registered. The only way *those* dogs could have been registered is if their parents were registered and so on.

In order for a breed to have been accepted by one of the registering agencies in the first place, the supporters of that breed had to provide credentials certifying that their dogs had been bred true to form and free of *out-crosses* (introductions of other breeds) for at least five generations. Before a breed is given official recognition, the supporters of the breed, often organized into a *sponsoring club,* are also required to submit a written description of the breed that gives a word picture of both what the breed should look like and how it should interact with humans.

The Federacion Cynologique International

The Federacion Cynologique Internationale (FCI), the purebred dog governing body for most of Europe and South America, recognizes well over 300 distinct breeds of dogs. Canine historians categorize them all as having descended from either one or a combination of four major groups: the Mastiff group, the Northern group, the Greyhound group, and the Dingo group. All four of these categories of dogs can be traced directly back to the wolves.

If you're interested in reading the AKC breed standard for any of the breeds, you can do so online at the AKC Web site at www.akc.org/breeds/recbreeds/list.cfm. Or check out *The Complete Dog Book,* 19th Edition Revised, written by the staff of the American Kennel Club and published by IDG Books Worldwide, Inc. This book is the most comprehensive resource on the AKC breeds, providing the official standards for every breed, in addition to tips on health, registry, and training of dogs.

Knowing the purpose of the breed standard

Breed standards are important not only for purposes of showing dogs, but also so that prospective owners know what to expect, and can be confident that their dog will meet the standard. If you had in mind a laid-back dog like a Basset Hound and, upon bringing the dog home, found that the dog behaved like an electrified wildcat instead, you'd understandably be upset. Likewise, if you brought home a German Shepherd to guard the family jewels, and she met intruders at the door with her tail wagging and a roadmap to the safe in her mouth . . . you see my point. Breed standards give you an idea of what to expect, and proper breeding ensures that dogs meet these standards.

Most breed standards tell you how tall (when measured from the shoulder to the ground) the average dog of the breed you are considering will grow. Some standards also give the average weight.

No breed has dogs of a "teacup" size. The term *teacup* usually indicates that the dog is a runt, possibly malformed or malnourished. Dogs advertised as "king size" or intentionally bred to be significantly larger than what the given breed standard recommends fare no better because skeletal problems often exist.

Taking a look at the breed standard for Boxers

Everything in the Boxer's history, including the first standard for perfection of the breed, developed in Germany, demands that the Boxer be bold, courageous, and protective. Yet standing right alongside those requirements are demands that the Boxer be peaceable and of good nature — cooperative and possessed of a willingness to learn and to abide by a master's wishes. Unless a Boxer combines all of these qualities in its makeup, the essence of the breed is lost. However, if balance is achieved, you have a portrait of the ideal Boxer.

Many breeds have changed drastically in both form and temperament from the original concept that the first breeders had in mind. Dedicated Boxer breeders throughout the world have made every effort to maintain the essence of their breed. A truly outstanding Boxer is respected and appreciated anywhere he goes — truly an international citizen.

If there is anything that truly distinguishes a Boxer from all other breeds, it is the unique construction of the Boxer's head. You can't possibly mistake a Boxer for any other breed if the individual dog being viewed has a head that meets the description in the breed standard.

Think of the Boxer's outline as a square. His height at the shoulder should equal his body length from chest to buttocks. The correctly made and conditioned Boxer, much like the prize fighter from whence the breed may have acquired its name, should be made of muscle and possess an "up and at 'em" attitude at all times. Check out Figure 1-1 for an illustration of the external features of the Boxer.

Temperament is a two-way street. A well-bred Boxer puppy comes to you with a sound and stable temperament, but you must return the efforts of the breeder by making sure your puppy is properly socialized and given the proper amount and kind of training. Otherwise, you are not living up to your responsibility — a responsibility any good breeder will expect you to meet.

Even though Boxers have a very precise breed standard, those of us who own and love these dogs probably think of the breed in a slightly less formal way. To capture the breed's physicality, think of a mound of Jell-O bound together with rubber bands. Strange as that may sound, I can't think of any other way of describing the twists and turns, shimmies and wiggles a Boxer goes through when he's happy!

Figure 1-1:
The external features of the Boxer set the breed apart from all other breeds.

TECHNICAL STUFF

The white Boxer

According to AKC standards, all white or even predominantly white Boxers cannot be shown at AKC shows. This rule is not based upon whim or prejudice against the white color. Instead, the color's ban from the show ring and the American Boxer Club's attempts to discourage breeding from white Boxers are based upon scientific research aimed at protecting the breed.

Here, Calvin D. Gruver, Ph.D., explains the reasons behind the American Boxer Club's position:

> During World War I, the Boxer proved to be a very reliable guard dog on the German front lines. The Boxer's true calling seemed to be as a dog of action. Its ancestors for centuries had been big-game hunters, and many of the features bred into those earlier dogs could be used in guard dogs: courage, toughness, strength, excellence in tracking, and so on. Even the Boxer's deeply instinctive characteristic of biting and holding the prey in a vise-like grip was useful in a guard dog.

> After World War I, members of the German Boxer Club began a campaign to get the Boxer officially recognized by state governments as a police dog. In 1921, three members successfully guided their Boxers through the difficult police dog tests. Then, in 1924, Bavarian police officials gave official recognition to the Boxer as an acceptable breed for police work. The Boxer had successfully transitioned from a general pet to a working service dog.

A year later, in 1925, the German Boxer Club declared white Boxers no longer acceptable for registration because police regulations forbade white dogs. From that time on, with a brief exception in Germany in the 1930s, the white Boxer has been unacceptable in every Boxer standard in the world.

In all respects except color, the white Boxer is the same as any other Boxer, and many white Boxers have made wonderful and beloved pets. But the white color creates problems for responsible breeders. The percentage of white Boxers with health problems is much higher than the pigmented Boxer, and no responsible breeder wishes to sell or produce dogs that may later cause grief for their owners. Colored Boxers themselves have occasional health problems. But white Boxers have those problems in addition to the unique problems created by a lack of pigmentation, including sunburn and skin problems. White Boxers are also more susceptible to hearing loss than their colored brothers and sisters (deafness results when the lack of pigmentation in the skin and hair deep in the ear causes nerve cells to die, usually a month or two after the puppy is born).

No responsible breeder would ever use a white Boxer in breeding or help obtain an AKC registration slip for a white Boxer. Indeed, the members of the American Boxer Club have agreed to impose strict disciplinary measures upon any member who does either of those things.

The Boxer's Role As Family Pet

The Boxer's agility, intelligence, and willingness to please combine to make the breed an excellent choice for any dog owner. Boxers excel in obedience programs, hospital therapy volunteer work, search and rescue work, Schutzhund training (involving tracking, obedience, and protection), tracking tests, and agility competition, and they make excellent watchdogs as well.

 But any dog with the energy and enthusiasm of the Boxer needs to have an outlet for all that energy, in order to avoid having those qualities take off in the wrong direction.

Does your Boxer have to fit the breed standard?

If you find yourself asking whether your dog has to fit the breed standard, the answer is both yes and no. Breed standards are guidelines. Because nothing in nature is ever perfect, these guidelines are really like carrots dangled in front of a good breeder's nose — perfection is something to strive for. The best results of a breeder's efforts, the dogs who most closely meet the breed standard, are the ones the breeder uses to perpetuate the line. These top-quality dogs also often become show stock. They are the dogs who are campaigned to become champions and appear on all those televised dog shows.

The other dogs are the ones who fall just a bit too short of this elusive perfection to act as candidates for either show stock or breeding stock. They are the Boxers, both male and female, who are intelligently bred and of perfect temperament but who just aren't that close to perfection.

A highly reputable breeder will give you the assurance that the puppy or young adult you buy will meet the highest standards for temperament and soundness in that breed. Temperament and soundness must be your highest priorities when you purchase a Boxer. Minor cosmetic shortcomings do not change the breed's compatibility or temperament. After all, you're planning to live with this dog for many years. A blemish here or there is not going to make an iota of difference. But the dog's temperament will.

If you're interested in buying a Boxer who you will also want to show or one who is suitable for breeding, in addition to being a family pet, you have unique requirements. Discuss this with the breeder so that he or she can help you choose a puppy that qualifies both temperamentally *and* physically.!"

Ginger: Loyal to the core

My family's first Boxer, Ginger, helped raise my younger brother and sister and was their constant playmate. Back in those days, leaving children out on the front lawn in their playpens while their mother did housework was perfectly safe. My mother did exactly that with my little sister Mary Ann. If she would have had any safety concerns, they were completely alleviated by Ginger, who stood guard over her little charge with unswerving loyalty.

All the neighborhood children were allowed to gather around Mary Ann, but we used to get a great charge out of the many ways Ginger devised to keep herself between any adult who wasn't a part of our family and the precious little girl. Ginger never threatened anyone — she never had to. She just kept herself in the way long enough that no one ever got closer than six feet from her little pal. She did a lot of tail wagging, but she was intent at keeping people at their proper distance.

On the other hand, Ginger was no pushover either. She proved her willingness to rise to the occasion more than once. One incident that I remember very clearly happened when Mary Ann was about five years old — that age when the word *bedtime* has about the same ring to it *castor oil*.

Our Uncle Steve was baby-sitting for us and made several attempts to get Mary Ann to head off to slumberland. Mary Ann not only refused, but, like so many children at that age are capable of doing, made it clear she wasn't about to respond to her baby-sitter's gentle requests.

Finally, in sheer exasperation, Steve took my sister by the scruff of the neck and headed her toward her room. Mary Ann reacted to this like she was about to be murdered. Ginger, who had been fast asleep on the other side of the room, awakened and came across the room in one lightning leap.

In an instant, Steve's shirtsleeve dangled around his wrist and Ginger had planted herself firmly between Steve and her adored Mary Ann. No growling, no further advances or shows of aggression. But her message was clear: "Hands off!"

Chapter 2

Is a Boxer Right for You?

A well-bred and well-trained Boxer has qualities that have made the breed one of the most highly regarded family dogs in the world. But remember: The operative words here are *well-bred* and *well-trained.* Far too many would-be Boxer owners fulfill their dreams of Boxer ownership by rushing down to the local mall and buying the first puppy they see advertised as "100 percent pedigreed pure Boxer." Unfortunately, these well-meaning folks don't stop to consider the temperament and constitution of the *parents* of the pup. Nor do they think about how willing they are to cope with a Boxer who hasn't had the benefit of an owner committed to giving the dog the care and training she requires.

If more prospective owners took the time to investigate the Boxer's history and understood the kind of owner a dog of this zest for life requires, they might reconsider their decision, saving themselves and a Boxer much undue stress. On the other hand, for the person who does the research and understands the Boxer's high level of enthusiasm, his temperament, and his need for space, no better choice than the Boxer exists. Of all the breeds I have lived with and known in my lifetime, I can honestly say that none has a greater capacity to learn or to be a better pal to their owner and their owner's family than the Boxer.

Having a 50- to 60-pound juvenile delinquent on your hands is not always the fun and games it appears to be from afar. The best way to avoid being in that regretful situation is to be sure — very sure — that the Boxer is the right dog for you and that *you* are the right owner for the breed.

Just because *I* think the Boxer is a fantastic dog doesn't mean that a Boxer is the right dog for you. And making the decision to get a dog — *any* dog — isn't one that you should treat lightly. So this is the place to do some serious soul-searching. This chapter allows no room for anything less than honest, thoughtful answers. The only ones who stand to lose out if you're less than honest with yourself are you and your dog.

Deciding Whether You're Ready for a Dog

Before you dash out to buy a Boxer, you need to take the time to carefully consider whether you're ready for *any* dog. Too often, well-intentioned people think only of the positive aspects of dog ownership — bringing home an adorable puppy, having a loyal friend at their side, playing fetch with a friendly pal. And these are all great benefits of owning a dog. But, as with anything in life, the benefits don't come without costs. So take a look at the following sections to get a reality check on dog ownership. If you finish reading the section and remain undeterred in your desire to own a dog, you won't be disappointed.

Looking at your past experience

Think about your experiences with pets, whether Boxer or Beagle, dog or cat. Was your experience a positive one? Have you ever owned a pet before? Have you ever lived in a home with a pet who was cared for by someone else (for example, did you grow up with a pet who your parents cared for)? If you can, talk with family and friends who own dogs and get a feel from them what the positives and negatives of dog ownership are. Your past experiences can either be great preparation for dog ownership, or they can leave you wondering what you've gotten yourself into (especially if your only experience with pets is watching Eddie on the TV show *Frasier*).

Getting real about your willingness to commit

When you become a dog owner, the dog will be there, in your home, all day, every day. Your dog will rely entirely upon you for his care and comfort. And don't forget that your dog needs to be trained — that is, if you want to protect your sanity and the sanity of those you live with.

Pets can't grab a snack out of the refrigerator when they're hungry. They don't have the slightest desire to clean up their own messes. And if they require exercise, they aren't able to hire a personal trainer. All of those chores are *your* responsibility.

There are as many different sizes and shapes of pets as there are sizes and shapes of people. I have friends who seem bound and determined to have at least one representative of every imaginable animal species in the world. What's more, they seem to thrive on all the work required to maintain the menagerie. I have other friends who find having to feed a canary once a day or throw a handful of cedar shavings into the hamster cage a time constraint. Know which end of the creature care spectrum you call home. If watering your plant seems like a hassle, you might be better off getting a cactus than owning a dog.

If your plan is to hire someone to feed, walk, and train your dog, and you just want a dog around so you can have some ears to scratch every now and then, save yourself the time, the aggravation, and the money, and visit an animal shelter once or twice a month to play with dogs who are in great need of love and attention.

Considering others with whom you share a home

If getting a dog is *your* idea, don't rely upon someone else in the household to step in and help (unless they have already volunteered to do so, without any arm-twisting on your part). Otherwise you may be disappointed — and more than a little frazzled — as you try to take care of your new dog on your own.

If you have children who promise, promise, *promise* that they'll walk and feed a dog every day, encourage them in their desire for responsibility, but don't count on it! It's not that kids are lying about their desire to take care of a dog. Most likely, when they say that they'll help, they actually mean it. But as you know, what's the most important thing in the world to your kids today is often forgotten tomorrow. Only get a dog for your kids if *you're* prepared to do the work involved in caring for the animal. And if the kids live up to their word and help out, it's just icing on the cake.

Figuring Out Whether a Boxer Is the Right Breed for You

When you've determined that you are, in fact, ready to buy a dog, your next job is to figure out whether a Boxer is the breed for you. With 148 breeds to choose from, you owe it to yourself and your future dog to be sure that you're picking a breed that will fit well into your lifestyle.

Being honest with yourself

To help you figure out whether you and a Boxer would make a good match, I've come up with eight questions for you to ask yourself. So grab a pencil and piece of paper, or sit in front of your computer, and write your responses to the following questions.

Don't just answer these questions in your mind; it's easier to overlook the reality of your responses when they're not in front of you in black and white.

Answer these questions with complete honesty. There's no sense in fudging your responses, because you'll only end up being frustrated when you bring home the wrong dog.

- ✔ Does the person who will actually care for your Boxer really want a dog?
- ✔ Is everyone you live with as anxious as you are to have a Boxer in the home?
- ✔ Does your lifestyle allow the time for the Boxer's care, training, and exercise?
- ✔ Is your living environment suitable for a dog of this size (at least 50 to 60 pounds when he's full-grown)?
- ✔ Do you have the endless patience required for your Boxer's training regimen?
- ✔ Are you physically strong enough to handle a full-grown Boxer?
- ✔ Is your own character and personality strong enough to establish the proper relationship between you and a Boxer?
- ✔ Can you afford the cost of Boxer ownership (this means *everything*, including purchase, upkeep, veterinary care, and food)?

If you answered no or even with hesitancy to any of these questions, a Boxer is not for you. Boxers are wonderful dogs, but they require time, patience, some degree of physical strength, a strong personality (someone who isn't afraid to intelligently discipline), and financial resources. If you think you may be missing one of these important traits, look for another breed.

Consult *The Complete Dog Book,* 19th Edition Revised, written by the staff of the American Kennel Club and published by IDG Books Worldwide, Inc., for great information on every breed recognized by the AKC. Just because a Boxer may not be the right dog for you doesn't mean there isn't another breed out there that will be perfect for you and your family. With 148 breeds to choose from, you're practically guaranteed to find one that's right for you.

Being realistic about Boxers

If you believed what you read in some of the dog books written today, you would swear that some breeds can do all that needs doing. People who love their dogs, particularly those who are crazy about Boxers, would have you believe that a Boxer is the one breed that can do it all, plus eliminate your need for a security system and help your kids with their algebra homework on the side. No dog — including the Boxer — can do anything of the kind.

In fact, your brain-trust Boxer won't be inclined to do anything outside of misbehave, unless he has the benefit of a leader who can teach him what to do and when to do it. Boxer puppies have a great capacity to learn, but remember that it's a *capacity* to learn. Boxers do *not* come preprogrammed.

Don't have unrealistic expectations of your dog. Your puppy will arrive with a blank slate, and the only writing that will appear on it is what *you* write or what the puppy writes without your direction.

Bring a new puppy into your home with the same attitude you would have if you were bringing home a human baby. You have to be on call for everything, providing both sustenance and comfort for your pup. So don't get a puppy the week before you head out of town for spring break. Choose a time when you'll be available to devote this kind of attention to your dog. Vacation time is great, as long as you're planning to be home. Or if you can't do it when you're on vacation, at least pick a time when you're not busy with other responsibilities.

Putting It All Together

So you've gotten real with yourself, posed some tough questions and given some honest answers. And you're still confident that a Boxer is the right dog for you. In this section, I cover some often overlooked topics to consider before you bring home a dog. This is your last shot, in this chapter at least, to consider possibilities other than Boxers.

What happens to your dog while you're away at work?

If you live alone, you're probably very much aware that your new Boxer will be your responsibility. And you may be completely prepared to spend your free time training your puppy and helping him grow into a wonderful adult dog. But on the other hand, if you live alone, you probably have to trudge off to work every day so that you can earn the money to keep in stock a full supply of dog biscuits. If that's the case, who will sit and hold your tan tornado's ever-growing paw while you're away?

Leaving your bundle of curiosity home alone all day will do nothing for his personality and even less for your furniture. A young Boxer left home alone day after day will lack the very thing he or she needs most: human companionship. A Boxer cannot survive without the companionship of a human being. The ones that *do* survive are bound to become neurotic and terrified of everyone except their owners.

Boxer pups have a huge storehouse of energy that they must use up in the course of a day. They can use all this energy constructively (with exercise and games) or destructively (by snacking on your shoe collection or excavating for lost treasures in the middle of your antique Persian rug). Be sure your puppy always has plenty of toys to play with.

So if you live alone, or if you live in a family in which everyone is gone all day at work or school, you need to be sure that you (and your family) have a strong enough desire to make the necessary commitment that dog ownership entails. And part of that, if you're away all day, includes finding someone to watch over your little angel when you aren't there.

How do the other members of your family feel about getting a dog?

If you share your life with a significant other or an entire family, you have to take into consideration their opinions, counting them just as heavily as you do your own, if not more. Your significant other may not be remotely interested in having your twosome become a threesome. And if that's the case, adding a dog to the mix will only cause friction in your home, and that's not the kind of atmosphere you want to bring a puppy into.

Ideally, you want every member of the family — especially the adults — to be enthusiastic about getting a dog. That way you can share the responsibility for caring for the dog instead of allowing the burden to fall onto one person.

Are you willing to train a new dog?

Training takes time and a huge amount of patience. You should train your puppy every day, whether it happens before work, after work, or on your lunch break. Not feeling up to it doesn't count. When it comes to puppies, you're *required* to feel up to it, because you can bet they're dying to spend time with you. Your state of mind has a lot to do with how well your training sessions go. So if you wonder whether you'll be in the mindset to deal with a dog every day, try a houseplant instead.

If you're prone to losing your temper, reconsider getting a dog. Taking your frustration out on your Boxer doesn't work. Boxers are extremely sensitive dogs. You may wonder how anything with such an extroverted personality could be anything but completely resilient. But all you have to do is yell a little too loudly at a Boxer and you'll see what I mean — your dog will be absolutely devastated. A properly raised and educated Boxer understands and accepts correction, but no breed tolerates abuse. If you subject your Boxer to abusive treatment on a continuing basis, even a dog with the best temperament in the world will be totally destroyed.

On the other hand, you shouldn't be passive in raising and training your Boxer. Boxer puppies have to start learning household rules from the very first day they come home. If you want your puppy to believe you and learn to avoid certain behaviors, the *no* command must mean *no* all the time, not just when your dog decides he wants to respond or you decide you want to enforce the rules.

Boxers have a tough time understanding the very human concept of changing our minds. If a mama wild dog were teaching her offspring to stay down in the den while she was off shopping for a venison steak for dinner, she would enforce this rule *all* the time. Rainy day exceptions wouldn't happen. And not a day would pass when she wouldn't feel up to correcting her little ones. You have to fulfill the same kind of responsibility with your pup if you want him to obey you like he would his mother.

Rule enforcement is one of the most important reasons to have a place to keep your dog when you're too busy to insist that the rules be obeyed. A securely fenced yard, a fenced and gaited outdoor run, or a fiberglass shipping kennel for indoors will keep your Boxer contained and out of mischief when you are involved in activities that distract your attention elsewhere or when you are out of the house.

Do you have the energy to keep up with a dog?

Making time for training is one thing, but your puppy also needs time to exercise. In order for your Boxer to grow and develop properly (both mentally and physically), he needs plenty of exercise. Think about children and the never-ending fountain of energy they all seem to be blessed with. Now multiply that energy by about six times and you have the activity level of the average Boxer pup.

Not only do Boxer pups have an *incredible* capacity for energy, they use it! Pups will either unload all those energy molecules under your supervision in some acceptable activity, or they will devise activities of their own. Believe me, what these little guys can think up on their own may make you wonder why on earth you decided to bring a dog into your life in the first place. Fashioning hideouts in the new sofa cushions, removing baseboards from the walls, digesting the contents of your most prized literary masterpieces — these activities are all ones that any self-respecting Boxer puppy has all the energy in the world for and needs no training to do.

Even the well-exercised Boxer pup may suddenly decide the time has come to redecorate the family room or help you get rid of all those shoes in your closet. (You can only wear one pair at a time, so why keep so many, right?) These activities are *fun* for your growing Boxer. Until the two of you have gone through all these activities together and you have convinced your young friend that repetition will *not* be tolerated, you'll need extra patience and money, to repair and replace everything your pup has left in his wake.

Can you afford the costs of owning a dog?

Beware of any bargain-basement price you see for the sale of a Boxer pup. There are always those people who are ready and willing to jump on the bandwagon and exploit a breed for financial gain. These people give no thought to the breed's health or welfare, or to the homes in which the dogs will be living. Highly recommended breeders, on the other hand, usually have waiting lists for their puppies. Even if there is no waiting list, no respected breeder would think of trying to *convince* someone to buy a puppy. Good breeders want their dogs to go to homes where the owners are already absolutely sure they want a dog. Expect to pay at least $800 to $1,000 for a companion-quality Boxer puppy from a reputable breeder.

The cost of buying your puppy is only the beginning. To that must be added the cost of fencing your yard or building a secure run so that your little pup doesn't wander off down the street. Then there are those costly trips to the vet for vaccinations, preventive medications, breaks, and bruises. Add to that the cost of enrolling in puppy classes, and the list goes on.

A Last Word on Boxers

If this chapter has discouraged you from owning a Boxer, then I've done my job. Because if reading about the reality of dog ownership is enough to change your mind, your experience with actually owning a dog would surely have been a negative one.

No one who isn't at least 110 percent sure that getting a Boxer is what they want should go through with it. The Boxer is not a breed for just anyone, and no dog should be purchased on a whim.

If you're aware of all the costs involved — financially and otherwise — and you're still enthusiastic about owning a Boxer, I'm thrilled that a puppy will be lucky enough to have you for his owner. The rest of this book is devoted to the great joy, challenge, companionship, and devotion that Boxer ownership entails. Taking home your very own Boxer pup, like the one shown in Figure 2-1, is one of life's great rewards, as long as you do so knowing what's involved.

Figure 2-1:
Resisting a face like this is difficult. But be sure you know what you're getting into before you bring any dog home.

Photograph by Phyllis Shaffer

What to look for in a breeder

You must purchase your Boxer from a breeder who has earned a reputation over the years for consistently producing dogs who are mentally and physically sound. The only way a breeder can earn a reputation for producing quality dogs over the years is by maintaining a well-thought-out breeding program. Responsible breeders rigidly select the individual dogs they will use in their breeding programs. Selective breeding is aimed at maintaining the virtues of a breed and eliminating genetic weaknesses. A great deal of time, space, and testing is required to effectively conduct a breeding operation of this kind, and all this is an extremely costly process. So responsible Boxer breeders protect their investment by providing the utmost in prenatal care for their brood matrons and maximum care and nutrition for the resulting offspring.

When the puppies arrive, the knowledgeable breeder initiates a socialization process. Only when these breeders feel the puppies have been given the benefit of the best care, nutrition, and sufficient human contact do they even *begin* to look for the proper homes for each and every puppy in the litter. They may keep one or even all the puppies in a litter until they are four, five, or even six or seven months of age.

The only way a breeder can continue to breed and raise Boxers in this responsible way is to charge a realistic price for their puppies. Naturally, a puppy with all these advantages is going to cost the buyer more than a puppy from a litter whose mother was never tested for any of the breed's genetic weaknesses or who was bred to a male of unknown mental stability. But could you even consider bringing a Boxer into your home who was not given these important advantages? A well-bred dog may cost more initially, but in the end that sound investment could save you thousands of dollars in veterinary bills and professional training to cope with inherited temperament problems.

Part II
Finding Your Soul Mate

The 5th Wave   By Rich Tennant

"I don't mind him investigating canine health issues online, I just wish he'd save his bookmarks, remember to log off, and quit drooling on the keyboard."

In this part . . .

*I*f you've already decided to get a Boxer, the chapters in this part are the place to start. Here you'll find great information on knowing what to look for in a breeder — because getting your pup from a reputable breeder makes all the difference. And I also let you know what to look for in a Boxer puppy. They all look cute, but here you'll get the information you need to pick the right one.

Chapter 3

Knowing What You Want in a Boxer and Where to Find It

*W*hen you're sure that a Boxer is the dog for you, and that you're the right owner for one of these wonderful dogs, you're ready to start thinking about what you want in a Boxer and where to begin looking for a dog. In this chapter, I guide you through the process of figuring out which Boxer characteristics matter to you. You consider everything from gender to age to personality type. Then, when you have a solid picture in mind of what you're looking for, I tell you how to go about finding your new best friend. I provide important information on how to find a reputable breeder. And I also inform you about the option of rescuing a Boxer who needs a good home.

Knowing What to Expect from a Boxer

Of the 148 breeds currently recognized by the AKC, virtually every one was developed by man to perform a particular function, and the Boxer falls into this category. In order to fulfill their duties, Boxers not only had to be physically built in a certain way, but they also had to have the character and personality to enable them to perform in their functional capacity.

Purebred dogs perform and behave the way they do because of generation upon generation of selective breeding. Expecting a purebred dog to behave against his basic nature leads to frustration for both the dog and the owner.

The size and temperament of Boxers can vary to a certain degree. Still, because of selective breeding over many generations, you can be fairly confident of what your Boxer puppy will look and act like as an adult. Most Boxer puppies will grow up to look like their adult relatives, and, for the most part, they will behave much like the rest of their family as well.

In the following sections, I let you know what to expect from the typical Boxer litter, in terms of size, color, and individual personalities.

Even within a given breed, variations and different personality types do exist. But you can be sure that, as an adult, your Boxer will have a joie de vivre unmatched by most other dogs.

Size

When you look at a litter of Boxers, you can be confident that all the pups will grow to be in the medium to large range of the canine size scale. You won't find any Boxers who fall at either extreme of dog sizes.

These are never carved in stone. Instead, they usually fall on a continuum. Your Boxer pup may grow up to be on the small side of medium or on the large size of large. You can be sure, however, that the dog will pack a good deal of muscle in that package, regardless of his size.

Color

You can expect a Boxer pup to be one of two colors: fawn or brindle. Some have white markings, and some don't.

Although they are completely ineligible to be shown in conformation events, white Boxers can make wonderful pets.

Individual personalities

Every puppy in a litter of Boxers has his or her own individual personality. So be sure to sit down and talk with the breeder you've chosen. The breeder is the one person who has been observing the pups as they have been growing. If the breeder you're working with is an experienced person, she knows best how to mix and match the pups from the litter with the right owner. One pup may need a Marine drill sergeant as an owner, but another pup may be just the ticket for the 90-pound weakling who just needs a gentle canine friend to lean on.

What's cute in a puppy isn't always cute in an adult dog

I have talked with first-time Boxer owners who delightfully boast that the puppy they picked was the biggest, toughest, and wildest in his litter. "Why, the rest of the pups parted like the Red Sea when he came on the scene," they brag.

This behavior may be cute for a puppy. But the problem is that the person doing the bragging is no more capable of learning to control this extra-extroverted personality than you or I are capable of leaping tall buildings in a single bound. I always make it a point to find out where someone like that lives, just to be sure that I am nowhere within 20 miles of the pair when their Boxer grows up and takes over the neighborhood.

Gender and Age: The Two Main Traits You Can't Miscalculate

When you're looking for the right dog, you can't always be sure exactly how big he'll grow or what his personality will be like down the road. But you *can* be sure of two things: gender and age. And you can gear your search accordingly, if you determine that you have preferences in either of these two categories.

Gender

Gender differences exist in dogs just as they do in humans. And, just like in humans, these differences aren't true across the board, for every male and every female. In my experience, Boxer females have a tendency to be more stubborn and independent than their male counterparts. When my females get something in their minds, they don't let go of the thought quickly. And they have the tendency to pay me back for some injustice, whether real or imagined.

My male Boxer, Raif, on the other hand, wants to be in the same room with me all the time. If I leave the room for a glass of water, he has to come along. And he doesn't demand my attention, he just wants to be with me.

Busy: A Boxer with little time for me

I had a female Boxer named Busy, who every morning in the summer pulled the pad out of her crate, carried it up a flight of stairs to the side of the swimming pool, laid the pad on a deck chair (I kid you not!), and then lounged there the entire day, without giving a thought to where I was or what I was doing.

When we went to the dog park, Busy coyly played up to the Golden Retriever and Lab males who were carrying a ball or a stick (they always carry a ball or a stick!). When she had the boys completely charmed, Busy snatched away their toys and all but ran them out of the park when they tried to get their own property back from her.

Although both the male and female Boxers are capable of becoming excellent companions and are equally trainable, take into consideration the male Boxer's larger and heavier size. Male Boxers have muscle power to go with their extra height and weight. So think about your own strength and size, and if you think a male might be a little too much to handle, opt for a smaller female instead.

The Boxer is a clean breed and relatively easy to housebreak, but the male Boxer (like the male of any breed) has a natural instinct to lift his leg and mark his territory. The amount of effort required in training a male not to lift his leg varies from one dog to the next. But keep in mind that a male dog considers everything in and around the household a part of his territory and has an innate urge to establish this fact. If your home is filled with expensive items, or if you're not sure you'll have time to train your dog not to lift his leg inside the home, consider a female instead.

Females, however, have their own set of problems, mainly in the form of semi-annual heat cycles, which begin when they are about one year old. During these heat cycles, which last approximately 21 days, the female has to be confined in order to avoid soiling her surroundings with the bloody discharge that accompanies estrus. Special *britches,* similar to diapers, are sold at pet shops, which assist in keeping the female in heat from soiling the area in which she lives. When your female dog is in heat, you must also watch her carefully at all times, to prevent males from gaining access to the dog and impregnating her. And don't expect the marauding male to be deterred by the britches, if your female is wearing them. A male will find a way to get past the britches to what he's after.

You can avoid (in the case of female dogs in heat) or reduce (in the case of male leg-lifting) a good many of these sexually related problems by having your Boxer spayed or neutered. Spaying the female or neutering the male saves you all the headaches of sexually related problems without changing the basic character of your Boxer. In fact, if there is any change at all in the altered Boxer, it is in making the dog an even more amiable companion. Above all, altering your pet precludes the possibility of the dog adding to the overpopulation of pets that exist worldwide.

One thing you can count on when it comes to gender is that every dog owner has his or her own preference. And those preferences are sometimes based on their individual experiences with various dogs. But sometimes, the preferences are there because that's just what the people have always known. Check around with Boxers owners who have experience with both males and females. Then make your decision based on what you've heard.

Age

Your Boxer's age when he first enters your household determines how you handle the arrival and what you have to deal with in the following weeks and months. You may decide that a very young puppy just won't work in your household. A young adult, a mature dog, or even an old-timer may be a better choice. (Don't discount older dogs. Often the older fellow who loses his loving owners and needs another good home to finish out those golden years makes a great companion.)

Like all living things, Boxers have different needs at different stages of their lives. They react to their new environment according to their age, and your job is to be prepared for this. In the following sections, I cover the various stages of a Boxer's life.

Avoid thinking of your dogs in human terms

All too often, people who purchase purebred pets say, "We're only going to breed the dog once, and then we're going to have Daisy spayed — after she has a litter to complete her development." Or owners of male dogs often say, "Fido needs a girlfriend to relieve his frustration." I assure you, neither Daisy nor Fido needs sex to develop or relieve anything! Actually, in the case of Fido or any other male, breeding only serves to *increase* his frustration rather than relieve it.

Birth to 7 weeks: In the nursery

During these first few weeks of life, a Boxer pup needs nothing more than she needs her mother and littermates. The mother and littermates provide sustenance, comfort, and warmth for a puppy (see Figure 3-1). During this period, the pups find out that other creatures do exist and they have to learn how to deal with them. In this stage, the pup finds she must compete for what she needs. Boxer mothers teach their offspring a great deal during these first weeks of life, so having this time with the mother and littermates is extremely important to a pup's development.

7 to 8 weeks: The diaper brigade

Around the age of seven or eight weeks is the perfect time to introduce a puppy to his new home. At this age, puppies are mature enough to readjust easily, but not old enough to have developed strong attachments to their mother or littermates. Puppies who remain too long as part of a litter instead of moving on to their individual homes can end up identifying with their siblings rather than transferring this relationship to their owners.

8 weeks to 6 months: The terrible toddlers

Just as with children, the toddler stage stretches on for a bit in Boxers. And it's not only the time that is stretched — during this time period, you'll wonder just how elastic your patience can be as well. Between the ages of eight weeks and six months, depending on the individual puppy, you may find yourself wondering at times whether your pup has taken leave of her senses with the nonsensical behavior and arbitrary balkiness she exhibits.

Figure 3-1:
In the first seven weeks of life, puppies need to bond with their mother and littermates.

Photograph by Richard Tomita

Just remember that everything in life is an experiment, a pup's curiosity is endless. At this age, pups find it necessary to pull electrical wires, climb fences, and test all objects to determine their chewability. But the Boxer pup is still dependent on you during this stage and wants to be with you all the time, wherever you go. His confidence begins to grow, however, and the early dependency that was so typical may diminish almost overnight. Work with your pup during this stage of his life, and train him to be a good canine citizen.

Though my male Boxer got through the stage with lightning speed, the female Boxers I had were inveterate thieves! Busy was a kleptomaniac, totally addicted to stealing refrigerator magnets and my reading glasses. She didn't do much of anything with either of these items, but I had to place them well above her reach when a guard wasn't on duty!

6 to 12 months: Rebels with (and without) a cause

This stage of Boxer life can be compared to adolescence in humans. Need I say more? When your dog is six to twelve months old, anything you can do he can do better — or at least that's what *he* thinks. Larger breeds of dogs, like the Boxers, grow quickly and mature slowly. So your dog may look like he should behave like an adult, but he's really not much different than a 6-foot-tall 16-year-old boy. His maturity may seem to manifest itself spontaneously, with no rhyme or reason. He may take awkward stabs at independence, only to revert back to his puppy ways when he's had enough.

I've found that some of the male pups become bashful and self-conscious at this stage (reminds you of preteen human boys, doesn't it?). Although I wouldn't call this behavior shy, some of the male pups temporarily lose that boisterous attitude that typifies the breed.

At this stage, you also find that what was cute when your dog was a puppy may be wearing on your nerves if it hasn't been corrected by this age. If those early bad habits haven't been curbed, you may have to deal with variable degrees of rebellion. This stage can be hardest on the males and their owners — what with the raging hormones. But these young rebels *must* understand clearly who is in charge (remember, that's you!).

Two to three years: The adult boxer (legal age at last)

The well-adjusted adult Boxer is confident and devoted, protective without being rash. If you adopt an adult Boxer who hasn't had the benefit of good training, you have some serious work to do. And if you've let your dog grow up without training him, you're beginning to reap what you've sowed for the last few years.

The geriatric Boxer: Silver threads among the fawn or brindle

Life expectancy for a Boxer averages about 8 to 10 years, and some Boxers live out their lives in a relatively healthy, vigorous condition. So defining when your Boxer will begin to exhibit aging symptoms is difficult at best. When your Boxer reaches this stage, however, she will have become pretty set in her ways — and if you've done your job, these should be wise and reliable ways. The old-timer may be a bit crotchety at times and not too inclined to put up with inconsiderate puppies and children. A Boxer's activity level slows down considerably as she ages, and the older dog may be experiencing the common symptoms of old age: arthritis, digestive difficulties, and bowel and bladder retention.

Finding a Reputable Breeder

Boxers are a popular breed, which means that you're sure to see ads in the newspapers advertising Boxers for sale, puppies at the pet store in the mall, and even litters at a friend's or neighbor's home. As hard as it is to believe, I have even seen what are supposedly "purebred" Boxer puppies being sold by a forlorn-looking little girl outside a supermarket.

But unless you buy your dog from a breeder who has proof that the parents of the litter have been proven clear of the breed's potential problems, you're taking a great chance that your dog may have health problems down the road. No one can predict the future, but buying your dog from a breeder who has taken pains to guard against potential disasters is at least some insurance that the puppy you take home has a better than average chance at also being clear of health problems.

When you buy a purebred puppy, buy only from an experienced and recommended breeder. And beware the backyard breeder.

Telling the difference between good and bad breeders

A *recommended breeder* is a person who has the sanction of their Parent Club (in the Boxer's case, the American Boxer Club). The recommended breeder is a member of the ABC and has agreed to abide by the code of ethics established by that organization.

So what's the difference between a *breeder* and a *backyard breeder?* Can't a good breeder keep his dogs in the backyard? If a breeder does keep his dogs in the backyard, does that mean the pups aren't any good?

These questions are all legitimate, but what you need to know is how to tell the difference between the legitimate breeder and so-called *backyard breeders.* Check out the following sections for ways to tell the difference between the good breeders and the bad ones.

Good breeders support the breed in numerous ways

Good breeders belong to Boxer or all-breed dog clubs and participate in many activities that support the breed. In the case of Boxers, just about every breeder I know is involved in showing or training organizations of some kind. The Boxer has such a great capacity to learn that dedicated owners feel as though they are negligent if they don't provide their dogs the opportunity to develop in this area. Participating on this level also provides the Boxer with the socialization and discipline the breed must have.

Backyard breeders do nothing else with their dogs except breed and sell. Their dogs have no special titles or accomplishments, and the owners do no training. They also don't participate in activities that protect the breed, like belonging to the American Boxer Club.

Good breeders are happy to let you see the environment where the puppies are born and raised

Good breeders are delighted to set up an appointment so that you can come and visit their home or kennel and meet their dogs. They want you to see their puppies and have a look at the environment in which the dogs are raised.

Backyard breeders may offer excuses as to why you can't see the mother or father of the puppies. They may tell you that you can't see the mother or father because the dogs "don't like strangers." Backyard breeders hesitate or refuse to take you into the area where the puppies and grown dogs spend their time, because these areas are usually unclean and in poor condition. The mothers and fathers of a backyard breeder's puppies are often not taken care of and aren't good with people. And that's not the kind of parents you want your dog to have.

Good breeders are knowledgeable about their dogs

Good breeders know a great deal about the dogs in their pedigrees and are ready and willing to discuss any of the problems that could conceivably exist in any Boxer pedigree. They also explain what kind of testing they do to avoid those problems in their puppies.

Backyard breeders are quick to assure you that their dogs "have no problems" and seldom know much about the genetic makeup of their dogs.

Good breeders interview you to determine whether you'll be a good owner

Good breeders ask you so many questions that you may feel like you're on a job interview — and you *are*. A good breeder wants to know whether you're ready for the job of owning a dog. He'll ask questions about your home, your family, and the conditions under which the puppy will be living.

Backyard breeders are willing to sell you a puppy with no questions asked.

The amount of time a breeder spends interrogating you as a potential owner of one of her puppies, in addition to the degree of her involvement in outside activities with the breed, are strong indicators of the health and stability of her breeding stock.

The following questions are ones most good breeders ask:

- ✔ **Why do you want a Boxer?** A good breeder wants to know what made you decide that a Boxer is the breed for you.

- ✔ **Do you have a home with a fenced yard? If not, will you or someone in your family be there to take the dog outdoors on a leash as many times a day as the dog's age and circumstances require?** Many breeders simply will not sell a Boxer to someone who does not have a securely fenced yard or kennel run.

- ✔ **Are you prepared to have the pet-quality Boxer you buy spayed or neutered?** Most breeders either require spaying or neutering before releasing a puppy's registration papers to you or they sell the pet-quality puppy with a "limited" registration, which will keep the AKC from registering any puppies that the dog ever produces. The limited registration discourages you from breeding, because if your dog has puppies, you'll have trouble selling them if they can't be registered.

- ✔ **Do you have children, and if so, how old are they?** Most breeders want to meet your children in order to get a sense of how well behaved they are. Households with children who do not behave well are not good environments for a Boxer to grow up in.

- ✔ **Do you have other pets?** Breeders want to know what other kinds of pets are already living in the home and whether these other pets are accustomed to strange dogs or puppies.

Responsible breeders aren't invading your privacy with all their questions. They're just extremely discerning about where their puppies go. Expect to answer a lot of questions about why you want a Boxer and how you intend to care for a puppy if they decide to let you have one. Get over the idea that you are doing a responsible breeder a favor by taking a puppy off their hands. If you get that impression from a breeder, find another one.

Good breeders provide their puppies with their inoculations and guarantees

Good breeders take care of inoculating their puppies and provide you with the information on which inoculations were given and when. They also tell you exactly when additional inoculations are due. Good breeders also provide guarantees for their dogs, detailing the conditions under which you may return the dog or puppy purchased for a complete refund and the conditions under which you may ask that the dog or puppy you purchased be replaced with another dog or puppy.

Backyard breeders may or may not have given inoculations or had health checks performed on their puppies. They don't provide you with future health recommendations for their dogs, because all they care about is making the sale. Backyard breeders provide no guarantees, because they know their breeding tactics often result in unhealthy dogs.

A good breeder usually tells you (without having to be asked) what kind of testing and what kind of guarantees they offer with any dog or puppy they sell. Always be sure that nothing has been left out and that you have not misunderstood what the breeder is responsible for providing you and your dog.

Testing for health and temperament are extremely important to everyone concerned with Boxer breeding and ownership, and virtually every experienced breeder does this testing in every generation.

Your breeder should conduct the following tests, to be sure the dog is healthy before he goes home with you:

- ✔ Tests and certification of the parents of the litter, establishing that the parents are free of hip and elbow disorders
- ✔ Appropriate eye and heart checks of the parents of the litter, to show that they are clear of eye and heart problems
- ✔ A veterinary examination of the puppy, revealing the current state of health of the puppy

Your breeder should also provide you with a complete list of all inoculations given (including the dates) and which inoculations are due (and when).

Considering the Rescue Option

If you're willing to consider getting a full-grown Boxer and don't have your heart set on a puppy, think about the possibility of adopting a dog who needs to be rescued. You may be able to find the Boxer of your dreams and help a deserving Boxer find a happy home in the process.

Many Boxers around the country need to be given new homes. The most common reason that any dog needs to be given a new home is that the person who bought the dog as a puppy didn't do his research and learn about the breed. When owners don't stop to think about whether a Boxer is right for them and whether they are right for a Boxer, they run the risk of learning the answer years down the road, and it often means that the dog is given to a shelter (if she's lucky) or put out on the street (if she's typical).

Most dogs wind up in the shelters because the former owner says she is moving and can't take the dog with her. Sometimes this is the truth, and sometimes it's just a lie told by someone who wants to get out of her responsibility as a dog owner. Before you adopt an adult dog, try to find out why the dog was abandoned, to make sure that he doesn't have any health- or temper-related problems

In the following sections, I give you some important information for places to turn if you're interested in rescuing an abandoned Boxer.

Rescue organizations

Nicely bred Boxers can become treasured members of your home, and they are often available through the many rescue agencies throughout the country. Just one of these organizations is the American Boxer Rescue Association (ABRA). Visit the ABRA Web site at www.boxerrescue.org/ABRA/index.html for more information. Or go to www.boxerrescue.org/Contacts.html to locate a local rescue organization in your state, province, or country. You can also write to the organization at American Boxer Rescue Association, 4412 West Kent Circle, Broken Arrow, Oklahoma 74012.

A good many other organizations manned by individuals who simply love the Boxer breed dedicate their efforts to rehoming Boxers. These individuals choose not to stand by and allow a Boxer to be euthanized in an animal shelter. Many of these Boxer rescue organizations or individuals have resources to trace the background of the abandoned dogs and observe the health, character, and temperament of each dog they place.

The more information you can get on the dog you're adopting, the better.

Humane Societies and animal shelters

Countless numbers of healthy, well-bred Boxers end their lives in the nation's animal shelters. (For this reason, responsible breeders insist they be given the first opportunity to rehome any dog they sell if the buyer is unable to keep the dog.) Still, many Boxers can be found in city- and county-run shelters. Check your local Yellow Pages under "Animal Shelters" or "Humane Societies" to find a shelter near you.

Passing up pet stores and classified ads

On more occasions than I care to count, I receive phone calls from friends who want me to help in their search for a Boxer puppy. Before I can even begin my search among responsible breeders, I often get a follow-up call from the same friend telling me that "the perfect puppy has been found!" Without even asking, I know the puppy has come from a litter bred by the neighbor down the street or by a friend of a friend. And that approach is good as long as the neighbor or friend knows what they're doing when they planned the breeding and as long as they're knowledgeable enough to help you select the right puppy. But more often than not, that isn't the case.

The same kinds of problems come up with classified ads in the newspapers and the sweet-looking little puppies you may see staring out the window of a mall pet store. Only there the unknowns are even greater. Classified ads can state what they want to state, but if you rely on the classifieds, you don't even have the recommendation of friends and neighbors to rely upon.

Sincere and responsible pet store owners do exist, but you can be confident that even among the pet store owners who are reliable and have integrity, very few are Boxer breeders. More often than not, the dogs sold in pet stores come from a source that the pet store owner knows nothing about. And that could very well be a puppy mill or a backyard breeder.

If you buy your puppy at a pet store, you have no way of determining the character of your puppy's parents. You have no way to determine what kind of care the puppy had from the time he was born until he reached the pet store. Even with a guarantee of the puppy's current state of health, you can't possibly determine what the genetic makeup of the pup will bring in the future as far as health issues are concerned.

If you're interested in adopting a dog from a shelter, investigating the background of the dog and finding out why the dog wound up in the shelter in the first place is very important. This information may be readily available at the shelter or it may take a bit of private investigating on your part to find. But take the time to find out as much as you can about a dog before adopting. You want a mentally and physically sound friend and companion, and many of these dogs are out there waiting for good homes.

Local Boxer organizations can often assist you in your search for information on a particular dog. Taking the time to investigate the dog's circumstances and history could easily result in your finding an outstanding dog who desperately needs a new home.

Chapter 4

Choosing Your New Friend

*W*hen you've decided where you're going to get your Boxer, the next step is picking the right puppy (or dog) for you. When you're faced with a litter of adorable faces, that decision can be a tough one to make. So in this chapter I guide you through the process, letting you know what to look for and what questions to ask.

Don't bring the entire neighborhood with you when you visit a breeder. This large number of people creates confusion and can be a distraction for the breeder, who has a great deal to discuss with you. Even if you have a very large family, you're better off making several visits with just two or three family members in attendance each time.

Knowing What a Healthy Puppy Looks Like

The Boxer puppy you choose should be a jolly, playful extrovert. Don't even think about taking a puppy that appears sickly, because you feel sorry for him and think you'll be able to nurse him back to good health. Nothing but heartache awaits you there.

Well-bred Boxer puppies with positive temperaments are not afraid of strangers. In fact, they love the world. So don't settle for anything less. Typically, if you kneel down on the floor and call the puppies to you, you'll have the whole litter in your lap before you know it.

Even if your puppy is eventually going to be entrusted with guarding the crown jewels, never consider a puppy who acts shy or suspicious of you. The pup also shouldn't act threatening or aggressive. The protective nature of the Boxer establishes itself at maturity, not when he's a pup.

No matter what kind of a future you have planned for your Boxer, chief on your list of considerations must be mental and physical health. The Boxer was bred to be an asset to his owners, and you shouldn't settle for anything less.

Be sure to observe the conditions in which the puppy is living. Just take a good look around. If anything seems unsanitary, you can bet your puppy has been affected. The puppy you select may smell perfumed and sweet, but if the environment in which the puppy is living is dirty and unsanitary, you can rest assured the perfume is just a quick method of compensating for the puppy's lack of care.

If one puppy in particular appeals to you, pick him up and ask the breeder if you can carry him off to an area nearby where you, the puppy, and the breeder can spend some time away from the puppy's littermates. As long as a puppy is still in a fairly familiar environment where scents and sounds are not entirely strange, the pup should remain relaxed and happy in your arms. Avoid any puppy who becomes tense and struggles to escape.

Taking a look at a puppy's health

Don't be afraid of offending a breeder by thoroughly inspecting your prospective puppy. Good breeders want you to be pleased with the puppy you select, just as they want to be sure that the puppy will be going to someone who truly loves and appreciates their dog. If you know what to look for in terms of general health, the breeder will be confident that you'll give the puppy the kind of care the pup deserves.

Body

Boxer puppies should feel compact and substantial to the touch. The puppy should never appear short-legged or long in the body. Don't mistake puppy clumsiness for unsoundness, however. Boxer pups aren't always the most graceful creatures in the world as they become accustomed to those big feet and chubby bodies.

Turning to the breeder for suggestions

No one knows more about the Boxer you are considering than the breeder of the dog. An experienced breeder not only has observed each puppy in the litter from birth, he also knows the important characteristics in the puppies — the things that set them apart from one another. Breeders know which puppies are the bullies and which are the crybabies. They know which of the puppies will require an exceptionally stout heart and firm hand and which of the puppies is more laid-back.

If you talk honestly with your breeder and answer all his questions, he will also know which of the puppies in the litter would be the best choice for *you*. That's why being straightforward with your breeder is so important. The bravest and boldest of the litter may come bounding out to greet you and may even be secure enough to give you a cute little "woof" to let you know your presence is being questioned. A winning personality? Perhaps. But this pup may also be showing early aggressive

tendencies that should be handled in a special way in order to raise a dog with a good temperament. Only the breeder can determine that for you. So rely on his help.

And if you're getting an adult Boxer, the same information applies. People experienced in the breed know what to look for when it comes to character, and although your first impression may be entirely positive or entirely negative, the longtime breed authority may know things about the dog you would never think to question.

If you trust your breeder when he says which pup he thinks would be the right one for you, you could easily end up with a dog who is an absolutely perfect friend and companion.

When you're working with a breeder, don't hesitate to share the fact you've done your homework. Breeders appreciate your interest and sincerity and they may even be more inclined to trust you with a puppy they think is particularly good.

Coat

A healthy puppy's coat is clean and soft. Boxers come in two colors — fawn and brindle. Fawn shades range from light tan to deep mahogany. Brindle color is actually clearly defined black stripes on a fawn background. These stripes can be very sparse or so heavy as to all but obliterate the fawn color behind them. Both fawns and brindles come with and without white markings. Color is strictly a matter of personal preference.

Conformation

Conforming to the breed standard is important even at an early age. Try to choose a puppy that represents the breed well.

A Boxer puppy should have a fair amount of bone, and his legs should be straight. The back is strong and level. The well-made Boxer puppy's muzzle-skull proportions are balanced. At this early age, the skull has a bit of a dome. Looking at the puppy from the side, the muzzle will appear to turn down at the end rather than up, as it will in adulthood. The jaw should be strong and broad. The ears may appear to be very large at this stage, but even the puppy who does not have his ears cropped will grow into them at maturity.

Fat puppies may seem less elegant than their more svelte littermates. And female puppies are finer in structure than their male counterparts.

All the reading in the world is not going to equip you to select a show puppy. That ability takes years and years of experience to develop, and even then, most breeders will only tell you a very young puppy has show "potential." If visions of blue ribbons dance in your head, seek the assistance of a breeder who has successfully bred winning show dogs over the years.

Ears

Check inside the puppy's ears. They should be pink and clean.

Ear cropping, if not already done by the breeder, is something that you and the breeder should discuss. The AKC standard for the Boxer says that a Boxer's ears must be cropped for show purposes. But the standard doesn't say that ears must be cropped if you *don't* plan to show your dog. This differentiation has created a division among Boxer breeders and exhibitors. Check to see if your breeder has a strong preference about ear cropping.

If you do not intend to show your Boxer, most breeders don't care whether you have your puppy's ears cropped. However, if the puppy is being sold to you as a show prospect, the breeder may insist you have the ears cropped if they have not already been done when you get the puppy.

Eyes

The puppy's eyes should have begun to take on their adult color by the time you bring him home. But no matter what, the eyes should be clear and bright.

Even very young Boxer puppies have a distinctly intelligent expression.

Mouth

Check inside the puppy's mouth. The gums should be firm, with clean white teeth. The teeth will meet either in a level or slightly *undershot* bite (the lower incisors may extend just slightly beyond the upper incisors). If you have any questions at all about the alignment of the puppy's teeth, discuss it with the breeder.

An adult dog has 42 teeth (22 in the lower jaw, 20 in the upper jaw). However, until a puppy is about three months old, he has only 28 temporary or "baby" teeth. Even with his first set of teeth, a puppy has 12 incisors. The incisors are the six small teeth in the front of both the upper and lower jaws.

Nose

A Boxer puppy's nose may not be entirely pigmented at this stage but will normally be completely filled in by the time he is mature.

Recognizing the danger signs

Just as important as being able to recognize the signs of health is the ability to recognize typical warning signs in unhealthy puppies. Here are some things to watch out for when you examine a pup:

- **Boniness, undernourishment, or bloat:** Avoid any puppy who seems bony and undernourished or one who is bloated; a taut and bloated abdomen is usually a sign of worms. A rounded puppy belly, however, is completely normal. Check the puppy's navel for lumps, which indicate a hernia.

- **Coughing or signs of diarrhea:** Coughing or signs of diarrhea are danger signals, warning you that the puppy is unhealthy.

- **Odor or discharge from the ears:** Any odor or dark discharge from the ears could indicate ear mites, which in turn indicates poor maintenance.

- **Runny nose:** A crusted or running nose is another sign of possibly serious problems.

- **Skin problems:** Skin eruptions are warning signs that the pup may be sick. Flaky or sparse coats can indicate both internal and external parasites. Although the puppy coat is thinner and softer than the coats of adults, the puppy's hair should not be sparse or patchy.

- **Watery eyes:** Running eyes can indicate any number of problems. Check to see if the eyelids are turned inward. This creates a condition called *entropion,* which is damaging to the eye and usually requires surgery later on.

Knowing which health-related questions to ask

You can tell a lot about a puppy by examining him yourself. But you also need to be prepared to discuss health issues with the breeder. The following sections cover the questions you should ask. ***Remember:*** These questions are ones any reputable breeder will be happy to answer. If a breeder seems annoyed or hesitant, move on to another breeder.

What kind of genetic testing has been done on the puppy's parents?

Although puppies are too young to have had any conclusive testing done for genetic complications, being sure that their parents have had these tests performed at appropriate intervals is important. The parents' good health gives a strong indication that your puppy has a good chance of following suit.

Although Boxers are no more prone to health complications than most other breeds, they do have their share of problems. (Ethical breeders breed against these problems by carefully screening their breeding stock, but nothing can completely eliminate health problems.) For example, Boxers are susceptible to hip dysplasia, heart ailments, bloat, some digestive problems, hypothyroidism, and both cancerous and benign tumors. Of course, not all Boxers or bloodlines develop these problems, but be sure to discuss these complications with the breeder. Ethical breeders will not hesitate to give you honest answers.

The parents of the litter should have been x-rayed to show that they are free of hip and elbow disorders. When this is done, certificates are issued by the Orthopedic Foundation for Animals (OFA) indicating so. Ask to see these certificates. A preliminary screening can be done on dogs at the age of 18 months, but a dog must be two years old before a final reading can be done.

When was the puppy's last checkup with a veterinarian?

The puppy should have been seen by a veterinarian shortly after birth and again by 8 weeks of age. If the puppy is much past 8 weeks, he should have been seen by the veterinarian again just prior to the sale in order to obtain a clean bill of health. Also, be sure that the sale of the puppy is contingent upon your own veterinarian giving the puppy a clean bill of health. Always have a veterinarian of your choosing look over a puppy before buying it.

What kind of guarantee does the breeder provide?

Ask whether the puppy will be replaced if he is found to have a hereditary fault. Discuss what kinds of faults and age limitations are included in this guarantee.

Any guarantees should be put in writing.

What inoculations have been given and when are the next ones due?

Although it is not at all unusual for puppies to have roundworms, you need to know when and if they have been wormed and what product was used. All of this information is critical so that you can take good care of your puppy when you bring him home.

Looking at a Pup's Personality and Behavior

Personality and behavior are just as important in picking a pup as making sure you get a healthy dog. In the following sections, I take a look at both issues and tell you how to find the dog you're looking for.

Personality

A big part of any dog is his personality. So when you look at puppies, try to find one whose personality will mesh with your own. A good breeder should be able to help you find one that seems like a good match to you. If you are the type of person who handles problem situations by waiting until they disappear, forget about owning the little bruiser in the litter who is bound and determined to be king of the hill. Though he may be appealing, that little pink-tongued cutie you bring home is a lot smarter than you think. And it won't be long before the little fellow figures out you are a *c'est la vie* kind of a guy or gal. Don't forget: The most laid-back Boxer in the world comes from a long line of party creatures, and if you don't set any limits, the average Boxer won't need long to turn your home into the canine equivalent of *Animal House.*

The experienced breeder will be able to give you a pretty good evaluation of the puppy you are considering. That person has been observing the litter since birth and has been through the growing-up process of Boxer pups time and time again. The breeder knows a great deal about what to expect from each puppy in the litter. If you give the breeder even a general idea of your own personality, he or she can help tremendously in directing you to the right puppy.

Behavior

Some of the key characteristics of adult Boxers are enthusiasm, energy, bravery, and devotion to family. By and large, you'll find these characteristics in any well-bred Boxer. But you can also look for the beginnings of these traits in puppies.

Although definitive temperament testing can't be done on baby puppies, certain characteristic puppy behaviors can indicate how suitable that puppy will be for you and you for it. ***Remember:*** The following characteristics are neither good nor bad. The same characteristic can be an asset in one situation and a liability in another.

Aggressiveness

Some puppies won't tolerate having their possessions tampered with and respond angrily or with biting. This response is usually directed toward litter-mates and seldom, if ever, toward humans. Uncontrolled aggressiveness is rare in Boxers, but if it does arise, this behavior must be dealt with at all costs. Try to avoid a puppy who seems unnecessarily aggressive. But be sure to know the difference between true aggression and playful puppy behavior.

Dependency

One puppy is always the first one out of the nest who rushes out to meet every stranger who comes by. Another may only do so with the other litter-mates in tow. The more dependent dog usually is more eager to please and easier to train. Whereas the more independent dog (the one who runs out of the nest first) may prove to be stronger-willed but may not need as much attention and reassuring.

Determination

Some puppies seem to have only one thing in mind and that is what they are trying to accomplish at the moment. Nothing seems to distract them. And others in the same litter can be redirected quite easily. How determined your puppy is will make a difference in how easy or difficult he is to train.

Dominance

How the puppy interacts with his littermates is a strong indication of how dominant or submissive a personality he will have as an adult.

With friends like this. . . .

Friends, many of whom have never even owned a dog, and who know absolutely nothing about Boxers, usually have all kinds of advice on how to pick a puppy. When the big day comes, the fewer people that accompany you to the breeder the better. You are choosing this puppy for yourself and those you live with, not for anyone else. If you think your tiny tornado will grow up to provide you with that macho, tough-guy image you've always wanted, think again. Joining a gym and setting out to become the next Schwarzenegger could prove far less expensive and less of a challenge than living with a Boxer you aren't qualified to train and handle. And taking home the forlorn and sickly little runt of any litter may well earn you a prize, but at best it's bound to be for spending the most money on veterinary bills.

What you should look for is a healthy, happy Boxer puppy who the breeder feels would be just right for the kind of person you are. The most easygoing, nicely adjusted pup in the litter is the only one you want to consider. If you use good sense in selecting your Boxer puppy, you'll have a friend whose intelligence and devotion will be everything the breed was intended to be.

Although a good part of how your Boxer behaves will be determined by how well the puppy is raised and trained, you can tell a lot by the way the puppy interacts with his littermates. But keep in mind that one brief visit may or may not tell you all you need to know about a specific puppy's personality.

Energy

Some Boxers play until all of their littermates are worn out . . . and then they're the first ones awake to start all over again. Other pups like to nap frequently and may be completely content to sit and watch their more silly littermates make fools of themselves for long stretches of time.

Keeping Track of the Important Papers

Before you leave with your young pup tucked under your arm, some very important transactions have to take place between you and the breeder. First, the breeder will want to get paid. Cash is always appreciated as is a cashier's check. If you make your payment with a personal check, the breeder may wish to have you come back to pick up your puppy when the check has cleared the bank. Don't be offended if this happens. Just think about it from the breeder's perspective. What recourse does the breeder have after you're long gone with the puppy if your check bounces?

On the day the actual sale is completed, you are entitled to four very important documents:

- A health record, containing an inoculation schedule for your dog
- A copy of your dog's pedigree
- Your dog's registration certificate
- A sales contract

These documents are all supplied as part of your new puppy's identification packet. They are the things that will make your little puppy a real Boxer and keep him looking like one. You should pay no extra charge for these documents. Good breeders supply them with every puppy they sell.

Health record

Most Boxer breeders have begun the necessary inoculation series for their puppies by the time they are seven to eight weeks of age. These inoculations protect the puppies against hepatitis, leptospirosis, distemper, and canine parvovirus. These diseases are all deadly and communicable (see Chapter 10 for more information). They can kill a puppy almost overnight. Even if the puppy escapes death, he will invariably be permanently impaired.

A prescribed series of inoculations have been developed to combat these infectious diseases, and obtaining a record of which inoculations your puppy has received and when they were given is very important. Make sure the records show the dates the shots were administered and the type and make of the serum used. This way, your vet will be able to continue with the appropriate inoculations as needed.

A puppy should never be taken away from his original home before these initial inoculations have been started.

A rabies inoculation is also necessary, but in most cases it is not administered until a puppy is four to six months of age or older. Local ordinances may have a bearing on when dogs need to be inoculated against rabies, and the rabies shot may be necessary before your dog is four to six months old. Check with your veterinarian, who will know what kind of regulations exist in your area.

The health record should also indicate what kind of veterinary treatment the puppy has been given since birth. This record will include details of the exams performed along with the dates and the type of medication used for each worming.

Pedigree

All purebred dogs have a pedigree. But the pedigree does not imply that a dog is of show quality. It is just a chronological list of ancestors — nothing more, nothing less.

Some unscrupulous dog sellers, who are attempting to gouge a higher price out of an unsuspecting buyer, lead buyers to believe that a pedigree has some special significance, that it indicates show or championship potential in some way. But this is simply not true. A pedigree only lists a dog's ancestors and authenticates the fact that all of the dogs listed on the pedigree are purebred Boxers. The dogs listed on the pedigree, however, may not have been show quality.

Rabies

The odds that your dog will be infected with rabies by another companion dog are highly remote. However, your Boxer could easily come into contact with wild animals, who are always at risk of contracting rabies. Do not overlook the importance of inoculating against this deadly disease.

The pedigree is your dog's family tree. The breeder and/or seller of every AKC-registered dog should supply the buyer with a copy of the dog's pedigree. The pedigree lists your puppy's ancestors, back to at least the third generation, by giving each of the registered names of the dogs. A pedigree is read from left to right. The first two names in the first column on the left of the pedigree are the puppy's *sire* (father) and *dam* (mother). The sire's ancestry, reading left to right, occupies the top half of the pedigree. The dam's ancestors appear on the bottom half.

In most cases, pedigrees are handwritten or typed by the breeder. These unofficial documents give you your puppy's ancestry, but like any document prepared by a human, they can contain spelling errors and other assorted mistakes. If you wish to obtain an Official Pedigree, only the country's official registration source (such as the AKC in the United States) can issue Official Pedigrees. The information contained in Official Pedigrees is taken from the respective organization's computerized files, as is the actual registration certificate. The registration certificate contains the address of the registration body from which the official pedigree can be obtained.

If anything indicates that one pedigree is better than another, it is the titles that the individual dogs in the pedigree have earned. Most of these titles are indicated on the pedigree and often in red ink. The titles and their appropriate abbreviations can be earned for everything from excellence of conformation to basic and advanced obedience accomplishments. Even if you have not yet decided what the future holds in store for your puppy in terms of shows, keep in mind that pedigree *titles* tell you that the ancestors have excelled in certain respects, that they represent true Boxer character and intelligence. Pedigree titles also tell you that the people who owned the title holders were responsible individuals who felt an obligation to help their Boxers achieve their highest potential.

Registration certificate

The registration certificate is the canine world's birth certificate. As with the Official Pedigree, the registration certificate is issued by a country's governing kennel club, such as the AKC. When you transfer the ownership of your Boxer from the breeder's name to your own name, the transaction is entered on this certificate. When it is mailed to the kennel club, it is permanently recorded in their computerized files and you are legally listed as your dog's owner. Two kinds of registration certificates exist, and I outline them in the following sections.

Litter registrations

In the United States, when a breeder submits an application to register a litter with the AKC, the information is checked. If the registration is accepted, the AKC issues individual temporary registrations for each puppy in the litter. Breeders have two options when they receive these temporary registrations: They can use the temporary registration to transfer the puppy directly to you, or they can individually register all the puppies in the litter in their own name first.

If your breeder provides you with a temporary registration slip when you buy your puppy, you must complete the slip and return it to the AKC with the necessary fee no later than one year from the date of the puppy's birth. (The puppy's birth date is printed on the slip itself.) Your breeder can let you know how to go about filling out the temporary registration and returning it to the AKC if you have any questions.

Individual registration

Most breeders like to insert an official registered name for the puppy on the blue slip using their kennel name as a prefix. A *kennel name* is the prefix or suffix used to identify the breeder or kennel that bred or owned the purebred dog. This name is registered with the AKC and no other dog may be registered with that name in the future. Most breeders add this to a dog's individual name so that it reads something like "Happy House Daisy" (where "Happy House" is the name of the kennel and "Daisy" is the name you've chosen for the dog) or "Roscoe of High Acres" (where "Roscoe" is the name you've chosen for the dog and "High Acres" is the name of the kennel). This way, the puppy is then permanently associated with the breeder. Actually, it is a compliment to the puppy if the breeder thinks highly enough of the puppy to ensure this kind of permanent association. After a dog is individually registered with the AKC, the registered name can never be changed. You can, of course, call the puppy anything you choose.

Sales contract

Reputable breeders also supply a written agreement that lists everything that he is responsible for in connection with the sale of the Boxer described. The contract also lists all the things the buyer is responsible for before the sale is actually final. The contract should be dated and signed by both the seller and the buyer. Sales contracts vary, but all assurances the breeder gives you in conversations and anything that is an exception to the outright and final sale should be itemized.

Be sure the contract you sign includes the following information:

✔ The contract should state that the sale is contingent upon the dog passing your veterinarian's examination within 24 to 48 hours after he leaves the seller's premises. The contract should have a clear statement of the seller's refund policy in the event that the dog does not pass the veterinarian's examination.

✔ The contract should list any requirements that the seller makes in terms of spaying or neutering the dog sold.

✔ The contract should indicate whether a *limited registration* accompanies the dog (meaning that the dog is not eligible to have offspring registered by the AKC).

✔ The contract should indicate any arrangements that must be followed in the event that the buyer is unable to keep the dog, regardless of the length of time that elapses after the sale.

✔ The contract should list any conditions that exist if the dog develops any specific genetic diseases at maturity.

The contents of sales contracts vary considerably, so you should read the contract carefully to make sure you understand what is included and what both you and the seller are responsible for. Figure 4-1 provides an excellent example of what a good sales contract can and should contain. A contract such as this one protects both the buyer and the seller.

Diet sheet

Your Boxer is the happy healthy youngster she is because the breeder has properly fed and cared for her every step of the way. All established breeders have their own experienced way of feeding and caring for puppies. Because they have been successful in breeding and raising their puppies, most breeders give you a written record detailing the amount and kind of food their puppy has been receiving. The breeder also usually gives you enough of the food the puppy has been eating to last until you are able to go out and purchase the necessary products yourself. Follow the breeder's recommendations to the letter, at least for the first month or two after the puppy comes to live with you. Following the breeder's established pattern reduces your puppy's chance of developing an upset stomach or loose stools.

Some breeders add vitamin supplements to their dogs' and puppies' diet. Other breeders are adamantly opposed to supplements when well-balanced and nutritious food is given. Be sure to clearly understand what your breeder's thoughts are on this issue and act accordingly.

PURCHASE AGREEMENT/HEALTH GUARANTEE

DATE _____
This agreement is made between XYZ BOXERS and the BUYER:

NAME _____ PHONE _____
ADDRESS _____
CITY _____ STATE _____ ZIP _____

for the purchase of the following Boxer:

REGISTERED NAME _____
REGISTRATION/LITTER # _____
COLOR _____ SEX _____ DATE OF BIRTH _____
SIRE _____ REGISTRATION # _____
DAM _____ REGISTRATION # _____

The above said Boxer is sold as a PET _____ SHOW PROSPECT _____ for the total price of $ _____. A deposit of $ _____ ($100 minimum) is hereby made and the cash balance is due to the SELLER before this dog is placed in the possession of the BUYER. Registration papers will also be held until the balance is paid in full. The BUYER understands that after a deposit is made, the BUYER has made a commitment to buy said dog and the deposit is therefore *nonrefundable*. BUYER will forfeit deposit and said dog may then be resold if the total price is not paid in full by specified date of _____.

IT IS HEREBY AGREED BY BOTH PARTIES THAT THE FOLLOWING CONDITIONS WILL BE MET AND THAT NO OTHER WARRANTIES OR CONDITIONS ARE EXPRESSED OR IMPLIED.

If this dog has been classified as a PET by XYZ BOXERS, it does not qualify as a SHOW PROSPECT (show quality) dog at the time of sale. A SHOW PROSPECT is a dog that goes beyond the definition of a PET (companion dog). This dog is not guaranteed to become a Champion of Record, but with the proper care and training on the part of the BUYER and/or handler, this dog should be a reasonable contender and do well in the show ring.

This dog is being sold with FULL _____ LIMITED _____ registration. (Limited registration means that offspring of this dog *cannot* be registered.)

XYZ BOXERS guarantees this is a purebred Boxer, offspring of the previously mentioned Sire and Dam.

The BUYER certifies that he/she is not acting as an agent for another individual in the purchase of this dog and will not sell this dog to any mass-producing kennel (puppy mill) or business.

(continued)

Figure 4-1:
An example of a sales contract that protects both the buyer and the seller of a dog.

The BUYER promises to keep the dog in a proper manner. It shall not be kept permanently in a kennel. If problems arise concerning keeping or training, or if the dog becomes seriously ill, the BUYER agrees to consult the SELLER. If it should prove necessary for the dog to change hands, the SELLER has prior purchase rights for a period limited to two weeks. Selling to a third party is only permissible after prior consultation with the SELLER, whereby the main consideration is the assurance that the dog is passed to responsible owners.

This puppy has been bred by XYZ BOXERS and has been carefully and painstakingly reared. The parent animals were mated with the aim of breeding good and healthy puppies. XYZ BOXERS guarantees this dog to be free of communicable diseases as appears to the eye at the time of sale. At the expense of the BUYER, this dog should be examined by a licensed veterinarian within 48 hours of possession to validate the Health Guarantee. (If purchased on a Saturday, this requirement is extended through the following Monday.) Should this dog be found in ill health, the cause of which is clearly attributable to the SELLER, this dog may upon written diagnosis from a veterinarian, be returned to XYZ BOXERS for a full refund of the purchase price or for another dog of equal value, the choice to be determined by XYZ BOXERS.

No other warranties are expressed or implied unless explained by SELLER below:

In the case of a puppy being sold as a PET, the BUYER will provide proof of spay/neuter by the age of 8 months, after which XYZ BOXERS will turn over full registration/limited registration to the BUYER.

The BUYER releases XYZ BOXERS, John and Jane Smith, and their estate from any and all liabilities and/or damages by fault of this dog after the time of sale. These damages include, but are not limited to, destruction of property and/or physical damage to any person or group of people. This contract is made out in duplicate, the SELLER and the BUYER each to receive one copy.

Signed
BUYER

_____ DATE _____

XYZ BOXERS (John or Jane Smith)

_____ DATE _____

The diet sheet should indicate the number of times a day your puppy has been accustomed to being fed and the kind of vitamin supplementation or additions to the food she has been receiving. Usually a breeder's diet sheet projects the increases and changes in food that will be necessary as your puppy grows from week to week. If the sheet does not include this information, ask the breeder for suggestions regarding increases in the amount of food you feed your puppy and when you should move your puppy over to adult dog food.

If for some reason your breeder doesn't supply you with a diet sheet and you're unable to get one, your veterinarian will be able to advise you on what kind and quantity of food to feed your puppy. So many foods are now being manufactured to meet the nutritional needs of all sizes, shapes, and ages of puppies and growing dogs that listing them all would be impossible. Like the food *you* eat, you get what you pay for. Turn to Chapter 9 for more information on feeding your Boxer.

Part III

Living with a Boxer

The 5th Wave   By Rich Tennant

"Oh, this happens every year around this time when the Hydrantgeas come into bloom."

In this part . . .

*I*n the chapters in this part, you'll get ready for your
Boxer puppy by having on hand all the supplies and
toys you'll need in the first few days. I also take you
through the process of introducing your Boxer pup to the
other members of his new household, including other
pets. And I give you some important and useful information on training your Boxer so that he's a valued and
well-adjusted member of your family.

Chapter 5

Preparing for Your Puppy

- -

In This Chapter

▶ Knowing which supplies to have ready when your puppy arrives

▶ Keeping your pup safe and sound in his new home

▶ Helping your dog lead a happy life by giving her safe toys to play with

- -

*W*hen you bring your puppy home, you will need all kinds of supplies and toys to care for your dog and keep him happy. And if you have everything on hand before your puppy puts his first paw down in your home, the homecoming will be much happier and more relaxed for both you and your dog. In this chapter, you get the lowdown on what you need before your puppy arrives.

Unfortunately, the one thing you won't be able to find in any pet store is patience. And that's the one thing you'll need most. When you bring home a puppy, you have to supply your own patience — and believe me, sometimes you'll need far more than you ever imagined possible. But always remember that what you give your pup in patience now will pay off in the form of a loving, loyal dog down the road.

The New Puppy Shopping List

If the puppy you're bringing home is your first dog, you probably need to start from scratch and buy everything on this list. If you've had a dog before, check to make sure that what you have will adapt to the size and needs of your Boxer puppy.

- ✔ A leash and collar
- ✔ Fences and partitions, to cordon off a living area for the puppy
- ✔ A fiberglass shipping crate or a metal cage
- ✔ Bowls for food and water
- ✔ Dog food, as prescribed by the breeder (see Chapter 9 for more information on nutrition)

✔ Brushes, combs, and nail clippers

✔ Shampoo made especially for dogs

✔ Toys

✔ Household odor neutralizer and cleaners

✔ Chewing deterrents

You can find all of this equipment at pet stores or larger pet emporiums. Many supermarkets now carry a very extensive line of pet products, and if you have the opportunity to attend a dog show, you'll find trade stands dealing in all of the products you will need.

In the following sections, I go into more detail on each of these items, so you know specifically what to look for.

Leashes and Collars

The collar you buy that fits your little puppy today will probably only fit around her wrist next week. Okay, maybe that's a bit of an exaggeration. But like kids do with shoes, Boxer pups seem to outgrow collars on the way home from the store.

Here's a list of the different collars and leashes you'll need for your puppy:

✔ **Baby collar:** Use this collar just to get your puppy accustomed to having a collar around his neck. You can find buckle collars made of soft leather or sturdy cloth and these work great as introductory collars. They are adjustable to about 14 inches, and even after the initial introduction period, you can use a baby collar to hold the puppy's identification and rabies tags for a while, until the dog outgrows the collar. Whichever collar you get for your puppy to wear when you first bring him home, make sure it's soft and lightweight. Your goal is for your pup not to even notice he has it on.

✔ **Training collar:** By the time your Boxer pup is three to four months old (when his basic training is about to begin), you'll definitely need a *training collar,* which is a metal linked collar used only for training purposes. Don't use a training collar as your pup's main collar or have him wear it all the time.

Instead of buying a training collar before you bring your puppy home, wait until your pup reaches the appropriate age and take him with you so you can be sure you're getting the proper size. The pet store owner will be able to demonstrate how to measure your dog's neck and how to put the training collar on your dog.

✔ **Lightweight leash:** The first leash you buy for your puppy should be flexible and lightweight. (Actually, you can survive those first few days by using a piece of light cotton clothesline if you don't yet have a leash.) When you first attach the leash to your puppy's collar, expect the little tyke to act like he's being pursued by a cobra. Fear not. Your little treasure will get over seeing the leash as a death threat fairly quickly. Avoiding a big, heavy leash will help your puppy get used to this foreign object trailing after him.

✔ **Leather training leash:** By the time your Boxer pup is three to four months old (around the same time you'll need a training collar), you'll need a leather training leash that's about four feet long. But unlike the training collar, which you should wait to buy until your pup is the appropriate age, you can start using a leather training leash as soon as your puppy has gotten used to the lighter weight leash.

Fences and Partitions

I strongly recommend creating a partitioned-off living area for your puppy's arrival. Paneled fence partitions called *exercise pens,* about three or four feet high, are available at most pet stores and are well worth the cost for confining your puppy to where you want her to be. Set up this area someplace where you and your family spend a lot of time, because your puppy will miss her mother and littermates very much and will almost immediately transfer this dependence to you and your family. Kitchen flooring is usually the easiest to clean up in the event of an accident, so if you and your family spend a good deal of time there, the kitchen may be the ideal place to keep your puppy.

This fenced-off area provides an area of safety for the puppy in addition to keeping her out of trouble. You can also use this area to protect her from being bothered (or bothering) older or larger dogs in the household, if there are any.

Confining your Boxer when he's outside

A securely fenced yard is the ideal place for your Boxer when he's outside. But if you can't fence your yard, or even if you just don't want to see your gardenia bushes transplanted every few days, a dog run can be a godsend. Some of the larger pet emporiums carry very strong portable sections of chain-link fencing, from which you can create any size run you choose.

An adult dog with seniority may not be entirely pleased with your new addition at first. Allowing the two animals to get to know each other through the safety of a fence is much safer for everyone involved.

Puppies who have not been raised with small children around may find them very frightening. Most puppies love children (like the puppy shown in Figure 5-1), but your pup may need a little time to get used to children and to feel comfortable around them. The fencing keeps the children at a safe distance and gives the puppy an opportunity to accept them gradually.

Figure 5-1:
Most puppies love children, like the one being cuddled in this picture. Give your puppy a chance to adjust to your kids, and they'll soon be the best of friends.

Photograph courtesy of Tracy Henrickson

Crates and Cages

I recommend placing a wire cage or a rigid fiberglass shipping crate inside the puppy's fenced-off area, with the door to the crate or cage open. The crate or cage quickly becomes the dog's sleeping den. It will also prove invaluable for both housebreaking and travel.

The crate is not a prison

When I have recommended crates to some first-time dog owners, you would think I had suggested locking their precious one in a trunk and throwing away the key. At first, some people see the crate method of confinement (especially during housebreaking) as cruel. But after new owners have gritted their teeth and done as I suggested, they invariably come back to thank me. The crate method is one of the most valuable training tips around. Using a properly sized crate reduces the average housebreaking time to a minimum and eliminates keeping the puppy under constant stress by correcting him for having accidents in the home. And there are always those days when everything and everyone in the household seem to be working at odds. The children need time out, you need time out. At those times, there is no better place for your family pet than in his very own little den with the door closed.

Most dogs continue to use their crates voluntarily as a place to sleep. Crates provide a sense of safety and security. The crate becomes your dog's cave or den, and in many cases it's a place to store his favorite toys or bones. The fiberglass travel crates are ideal for Boxers. They can be purchased from almost any pet store and even in some major supermarkets. Do check to see if the manufacturer's warranty states that the crate is "airline approved," however, just in case you and your dog decide to visit the relatives in Oshkosh. Even when you decide to have your Boxer accompany you in the car, he is safest in his crate.

Dogs learn to look at their crates as safe and private quarters. Those of us who live on the earthquake-prone west coast find crates are the place our dogs make a beeline to at the first rumble. With some dogs, we owners have to do a good deal of coaxing to get our dogs to come out of their "earthquake shelter."

These crates or cages come in various sizes. Even though the size that will accommodate your Boxer when he's fully grown may seem terribly oversized for him when he's still a young puppy, you'll be amazed at how quickly your puppy's size will increase in just a matter of weeks. So I recommend getting the size of crate that you anticipate your dog needing when he's fully grown.

For a male Boxer, buy a crate that measures about 26 inches wide by 42 inches long by 30 inches high. The next size down (24 inches wide by 36 inches long by 26 inches high) will be big enough for most females. Crates of these sizes will accommodate the average fully grown Boxer and will permit the dog to stand up and turn around.

If your Boxer grows well beyond the norm for the breed, giant size crates are also available. They typically measure about 28 inches wide by 48 inches long by 31 inches high. But remember, this is your dog's sleeping quarters, not his home gym. So as long as your fully grown Boxer has room to stand up, turn around comfortably, and lie down without being cramped, his crate is big enough.

Boxer puppies do not like to relieve themselves where they sleep, so if you're using a crate that's large enough for the pup to consider one end of it her sleeping area, you may find that she'll do her eliminating at the other end — a behavior that may be convenient for *her* but one you don't want to encourage. If you're using a large crate for your Boxer puppy, put a plywood partition up to reduce the inside space as much as needed. Or put a large box in the far end of the crate — just pick one large enough that your pup won't be able to crawl in. If that doesn't appeal to you, you can usually find inexpensive smaller crates at a local garage sale that may work until your pup is housebroken and big enough not to view one end of the crate as her private latrine.

In warm climates, some Boxer owners prefer the wire crates, because they provide better air circulation for their dogs. The wire crates come in all sizes and some have the additional advantage of being collapsible so you can fold them up flat if you need to transport them.

Dishes for Feeding and Watering

Any pet store carries a wide range of food and water dishes for dogs. You can get everything from inexpensive plastic ones to dishes made of stainless steel or stoneware.

I recommend opting for the stainless steel or stoneware versions, because your dog won't be able to chew them and knock over his food or water.

For more information on feeding your Boxer, check out Chapter 9.

Grooming Supplies

Grooming isn't just a matter of keeping your dog looking good, it's also a matter of maintaining your Boxer's health. Have on hand the following basic supplies, and you'll be good to go:

- **Stiff-bristle brush:** A stiff-bristle brush works well on a regular basis to remove all debris and loose hair from your Boxer.

- **Greyhound glove (or a thick piece of terrycloth):** These do a great job of adding the finishing touches and help make your Boxer's coat gleam.

- **Nail clippers:** Nail clippers and nail grinders work well for maintaining your Boxer's nails. Check out Chapter 10 for more information on using these valuable items.

✔ **Shampoo:** Bathing your dog with a good shampoo made especially for dogs can be done routinely. Dog shampoos are formulated so that their pH balance is set for a dog's needs, which are significantly different than yours and mine.

✔ **Dry baths:** A wet bath is not the only approach to getting your Boxer's coat clean. Try one of the many dry bath products that are extremely effective as well. These products are meant to be quickly rubbed in and wiped or brushed out, eliminating the mess and time involved in a wet bath.

A thorough five-minute brushing every couple of days will suffice most of the year but seasonal shedding demands daily brushing in order to keep the hair from flying.

Neglecting to brush your Boxer will cause her to drop every unwanted hair exactly where you don't want it to be. Your Boxer will shed a bit all through the year, and she'll go through a major shedding in the spring and in the fall. Females tend to have a major shed when they come into heat as well.

Toys

Boxers love toys and games. You'll seldom have any problem in enticing your dog to play, and when she learns a game well, she'll become a master at coaxing you into playing it with her, finding the toys herself if she has to (see Figure 5-2). The trick is in finding the right toys and teaching her games that are fun but that don't lead to complications or accidents. In the following sections, I cover exactly that.

Chew toys

Puppies have a strong need to chew. Puppies love chewing just about as much as anything else they do. Providing your puppy with fun and interesting chew toys will save a great deal of wear and tear on your furniture and your favorite pair of shoes. Plus, chew toys serve the important role of helping to strengthen a puppy's jaws.

But you have to be careful when choosing chew toys for your Boxer. What is safe and fun for your neighbor's Chihuahua could be swallowed or splintered (right along with the Chihuahua) by your Boxer before you can even say, "Call the vet!" Pet stores and catalogs carry all kinds of toys. Some toys provide hours or days of chewing pleasure, and others are not much more than a quick snack.

Figure 5-2:
This Boxer knows exactly which toy she's searching for. Always have a supply of safe and fun toys on hand for your Boxer to play with.

The dinosaur-size rawhide bones are good for Boxers, just as long as you keep your eye on the pup. Some puppies chew these rawhide bones for days. Other pups become masters at chewing off chunks and swallowing the pieces whole. The chunks can get caught in a dog's throat, so don't take the risk of leaving your dog alone with a rawhide bone. And if you notice him biting off large pieces instead of gnawing on it slowly, try another treat instead.

Cattle and horse hooves are enjoyed by Boxers, too, but the size of the hoof is important. If your big guy is the chew-and-swallow type, cattle and horse hooves aren't safe.

A big fresh knuckle bone is a great idea and your Boxer will love you for giving it to him. Just make sure the bone is large enough not to choke your dog.

If the thought of giving your dog the bone of another animal to chew on makes your stomach turn, you can find some great toys for your Boxer to chew on that are completely synthetic. These well-manufactured substitutes have different names, such as Nylabone and Gumabone. These synthetic bones are virtually indestructible and your puppy or adult Boxer can chew away to his heart's content.

Play toys

In addition to loving chew toys, your dog will be kept happy for hours with play toys. Kong toys are super-tough rubber toys that are all but impossible to tear apart.

Large Boomer Balls are made of nylon and can keep your Boxer entertained by the hour. These balls can be purchased at some dog show trade stands. They can be pushed and chased all over creation, though, so you're better off allowing your Boxer to play with Boomer Balls in a fenced-in area. Some dogs are so focused on the ball they don't realize they have chased the thing a mile down the road or into the middle of commuter traffic!

Rope toys are another great option for your Boxer. They take a tremendous amount of punishment before they give up the ghost. Rope toys are washable and come in all kinds of shapes and sizes. Because they're fun to shake and throw, outdoors is probably the best place for playing with them. You wouldn't want the rope toy to go flying into your objets d'art.

Toys to avoid

Don't give your pup an old sock or discarded slipper to chew on — even if it *does* save money. When your dog chews on an old sock or similar item, he won't be able to tell the difference between the old items that are okay for him to chew and the brand new socks or shoes that you bought last week. Everything you and your family wear or have worn have the same special smells, and your Boxer won't care that you bought those socks or shoes last week if they are accustomed to playing with the older versions.

Avoid giving your dog something that has been painted. The toy may be as colorful as Disneyland itself, but make sure that what makes that color is *nontoxic*.

Teddy bears and other stuffed toys are not a good idea either. Your Boxer can treasure and care for a favorite teddy bear for months on end, and then one day, for no apparent reason, the bear winds up inside your Boxer's tummy. When this happens, the three of you (you, the Boxer, and the bear) will all be at the vet's office facing surgery. Even before he swallows the bear, however, your Boxer is going to feel duty-bound to remove the eyes, nose, and squeaker from any stuffed toy.

Odor Neutralizers

Having a dog in the house, even a dog the size of a Boxer, does not mean the place has to smell like a stable — or even like a doghouse. And just because your Boxer has short hair doesn't mean that your home will be free of doggie odor either. All dogs have doggie odor — some more, some less. If you keep your Boxer's skin and coat clean, you'll minimize the amount of odor that is present. Realize, of course, that if your Boxer has the run of the house and you aren't diligent about keeping him clean and shiny bright, his doggie odor will be transferred to every carpet, every chair, and every bedspread he rests on.

As fastidious as you may be, sometimes doggie odors can just get ahead of you. Supermarkets carry sprays, candles, liquids, and plug-ins that help in these cases, but the pet stores often carry products that their customers have learned through experience really work better.

Chew Deterrents

A product called Grannick's Bitter Apple (it tastes just like it sounds!) is available at pet stores, hardware stores, and some pharmacies. It's nonpoisonous and can be used to coat electrical wires and furniture legs so that your dog doesn't chew them. In most (but not all) cases, Bitter Apple deters a puppy from damaging household items. I have also applied Bitter Apple to itchy spots to keep a dog from licking or biting himself.

If Bitter Apple does not deter your dog, you can buy plastic tubing at hardware stores, which can be placed around electrical cords and some furniture legs.

Puppyproofing your home

Your Boxer pup will not spend her entire life inside the partitioned area you've created, but her curiosity and mischief level will not necessarily diminish as she grows. Your puppy's safety and your sanity depend upon your ability to properly puppyproof your home. Walk around your house, picking up any items that your puppy could get into. But remember that what your puppy can't reach today, she'll be able to bring crashing down tomorrow.

Mouth-size objects, electrical outlets, hanging lamp cords, and a host of other things you never looked upon as dangerous can be lethal to an inquisitive and mischievous puppy. Think of your Boxer puppy as one part private investigator and one part vacuum cleaner. That way you will be much better equipped to protect your puppy and your belongings.

Buy ties to keep those cupboard doors closed. Ingesting a few sponges or the contents of any plastic bottle that can be chewed open are dangerous for dogs. Puppies can get into places that defy the imagination. Many cleaning products, gardening supplies, and medicines can be poisonous and must be kept in securely latched or tied cupboards out of your puppy's reach.

Chapter 6

Welcoming a Boxer into Your Family

*W*hen you first bring your Boxer puppy home, you may find your puppy-raising experiences could provide an ongoing script for a sitcom. As you've probably already begun to suspect, a new puppy is capable of finding her way into situations you never thought possible for any dog to think up, much less one so young. You've probably also begun to think that keeping ahead of all this is not much easier than training for the next Olympics.

Just in case you think you can eliminate all the problems of puppyhood by getting an adolescent or mature Boxer instead, forget it. Granted, you won't have the baby puppy problems, but you'll still have the problems a more experienced adolescent or adult dog will present.

Just remember that all this hard work is worth it. But I don't need to remind *you* of that.

Facing the Inevitable Facts of Life with a New Dog

Bringing a new dog of any age into your home presents transition problems, and these are problems that you'll just have to deal with. You'd have a good many of the same transition problems if you were bringing another human being into your home for the first time.

The most important thing to keep in mind when you bring your new puppy home is remember the two p's — preparation and, you guessed it, patience.

Use your breeder as a resource when you're dealing with a new pup. Not only does the breeder from whom you are getting your Boxer understand how Boxers react to most situations, the breeder also knows how your particular dog is inclined to behave. Believe me, having input on those two issues alone can save you a good many headaches. Keep in mind that everything in your home is entirely foreign to your new dog. To make matters worse, she has no familiar faces around to assure her that everything is okay. So beginning with the first day your new Boxer enters your home, try to keep in mind two very important tips :

✔ **Do not let your Boxer do anything on the first day or days that you will not want her to do for the rest of the time you're living together.**

If you allow your dog to sleep in bed with you the first few nights because she appears sad and lonely, don't expect her to be ecstatic about banishment to her crate in the kitchen a few weeks down the road. Feeding your puppy buttered toast while he sits on your lap through breakfast may be fun when he's just a tot. But where will he sit and what will he eat when he weighs over 60 pounds?

✔ **Never be severe in correcting unwanted behavior.**

Try to avoid nagging and correcting your new dog every time she turns around. New dogs, regardless of age, make mistakes. But they don't know the rules yet, so that's to be expected. Just avoid putting the new dog into situations where she will be breaking the rules. This way, you don't have to constantly scold her for getting into trouble, but you also don't ignore bad behavior — because it isn't happening.

Making It through the Difficult First Week

The first week is the toughest, especially for a very young puppy. When you take a puppy away from his littermates and put him into an entirely strange environment, he's going to be confused and lonely. No warm bodies to snuggle up to. No playmates for games. During the day is bad enough, but nights seem even worse. Thinking ahead on your part can help alleviate some of the transition trauma your pup will experience.

Making the trip home

The safest way to transport your puppy from the kennel to your home is to obtain a pet carrier or a cardboard box large enough for the puppy to stretch out comfortably with sides high enough so that he can't climb out. Put a layer of newspapers at the bottom in case of accidents and a soft blanket or towel on top of that. Ideally, another family member or friend should accompany you to do the driving or hold the carrier that the puppy is in.

Hold the box on your lap if you can. That way, *your* reassuring hand will be the first to stroke the puppy as he becomes accustomed to his strange and ever-changing new world.

Ideally, you should try to collect your puppy from the breeder in the morning so that the newcomer has at least one full day to acclimate himself to the overwhelming new world he is being thrust into.

Although not always possible, try to bring your puppy home for the first time when you or another family member has a week or at least a few days off. Being with the pup most of the time those first few days helps tremendously. After a week has gone by, your puppy will have begun to forget all about his littermates and will begin to become a member of your family, even if the "family" is just the two of you. If you can't manage a week off, try taking a Friday off and picking the puppy up early that day, giving you a full three days to get past that difficult transition.

Braving the first nights

As brave as your pup may have seemed in the midst of his littermates, he may be completely bewildered in your home. Expect some mournful sounding complaints the first few nights. Usually, with a bit of help from you, the puppy will settle in and sleep through the night after a few days. However, some pups will keep up the lonely crying and howling night after night until you, your family, and the entire neighborhood are ready to move to another country. You may be amazed at just how loud and how persistent a Boxer puppy can be when he wants to announce to the world that he is homesick and lonely.

If your puppy is having trouble sleeping through the night, try keeping him in a box next to your bed. This method has three advantages:

- ✔ Your puppy will not feel quite so all alone in the world if you drop your hand down into the box to reassure him.
- ✔ You don't have to get out of your bed on those cold winter evenings to do this.
- ✔ Your puppy learns to transfer his dependency from his littermates and mother to you.

Housebreaking your new puppy

Your breeder may have started a housebreaking routine with your puppy. If so, check carefully to learn just how this was being done so that you can follow suit. If your puppy has been accustomed to relieving herself outdoors, don't expect the youngster to understand that you want her to use newspapers indoors instead. If the situation is the other way around and you only want the pup to eliminate outdoors, take the newspapers with you at first and put them down where you want the puppy to take care of her duties. You can eliminate the papers later.

Everything is new for the puppy and every household rule has to be learned. Be sure everyone in your home understands being consistent with the rules is a critical part of your Boxer's early education. A puppy won't be able to understand that lounging on the sofa with the kids is okay but it's not all right when Mom is looking.

Solving Some Common Puppy Problems

Puppies, despite their adorable faces and cute pudgy bodies, bring with them some fairly common problems. And in this section, I let you know how you can fix those problems — or avoid them before they start.

Crying and whining

Human babies cry, and puppies are no different. Puppies cry because they're scared or angry, because they need something, and because they're anxious when left alone. Teaching your Boxer that he will live through the experience of being alone and come out of your absence perfectly fine is very important. Some puppies fret a bit and then settle down. Others are bound and determined that you are going to give them the attention they want.

Never let your Boxer get the idea that if she is persistent enough, salvation will come. When you teach your puppy that his crying will be rewarded by getting what he wants, life becomes a nightmare, because he'll start to apply what you taught him to everything he wants or doesn't want. Nip this behavior in the bud. The sooner you start, the easier the demanding behavior will be to correct.

Major: The strongest vocal chords on the block

When we were back East a few years ago, we selected a Boxer puppy for a friend and, due to unanticipated circumstances, we had to keep the dog most of the summer. Major was six months old and the owner of the loudest voice ever issued to a Boxer, I'm certain. He insisted that he was not going to be left home alone — ever! He made sure we understood this by howling at the top of his lungs for the entire first month he lived with us.

Finally, after amazing persistence on our part, he relented and all was well. Weeks later we had a dogsitter come in one weekend when we had to be away. Major evidently thought it was worth a shot, so he gave the sitter the same vocal rendition he had tried on us. The sitter responded by keeping Major at her side over the entire weekend. So when we returned, we were back at square one, and it took us still another month to correct the habit we had dealt with once before!

Begin by confining your pup to his crate while you are in the same room. Some pups will be fine with this as long as they can see you. Others may decide they can only be happy under your feet. If the puppy begins to whine or bark give a sharp "quiet!" command. Usually that does the trick. If not, you may need to rap the crate with the flat of your hand when you give the command. Almost invariably, the noise and simultaneous command will make the puppy pause if not stop entirely. You must have the last word and if you are persistent you will definitely win. Do not take the puppy out to comfort him. This is exactly what the pup is after, and you will be teaching him that the way to get what he wants is to be vocal about it.

Sometimes, with the more persistent little fellows, sterner measures are necessary. Purchase a plastic spray bottle or water gun and fill it with water, adjusting the spray to a steady stream. The minute the barking or whining begins, command "quiet!" and give the pup a quick shot. No harm is done, but puppies (and even grown dogs) hate this. A few rounds with the water treatment usually gets the message across.

Another effective method for puppies or barking adults is the shake-the-can method. A small aluminum can from a soft drink is ideal. Put a dozen pennies in the can and shake it. The noise is surprisingly loud, and if you throw the can at or near the puppy's crate, it will surely startle the complainer. (Never hit the puppy with the can, of course.) Be sure to give the "quiet" command first and immediately follow the command by shaking the can. When the puppy understands the consequences for whining or barking, you can start standing by in the next room. Just as soon as the racket starts, dash into the room and give your "quiet" command. Follow up with the water or shake-can technique if necessary, but make sure you intervene each time and always use the same command. Don't make the mistake of saying, "no" one time, "quiet" the next, and "stop" still another time. This inconsistency does nothing but confuse your dog.

Housebreaking

Most Boxer puppies get the housebreaking message right off the bat; some may require you to call upon all the patience reserves you have access to. By and large, the male Boxers I've had have proven easier to housebreak than their female counterparts. You just never know how much time your pup will need.

Boxers are basically very clean and, when they're dealt with properly by the breeder in their first few weeks out of the nest, housebreaking is a breeze. But accidents can and do happen. *Remember:* They're babies! Avoiding the problem is the easiest way to approach this particular phase of your puppy's training. When it's time to go, a puppy will be inclined to return to the same area he has relieved himself previously. If that's in the middle of your new cream-colored oriental rug, so be it. The puppy won't mind. But if the proper spot, with all the right smells, is outdoors, the puppy will begin to develop a vague yearning for that spot. He'll have a mild, sort of distressed expression and perhaps give a little whine, seconds before it happens. Take your puppy out often and to the same area of your yard, and she'll eventually want to return there, like the little pup shown in Figure 6-1.

Just call him MacGyver

Some dogs are determined not to be left outdoors alone at any time. A friend of ours exhausted every known method to keep his young Boxer from standing at the fence and barking. Finally, in desperation, he rigged up a sound-activated water hose system so that the dog received a good blast of water every time he began barking. The Boxer learned very quickly that the consequences far exceeded the pleasure of vocalizing his unhappiness.

Figure 6-1:
Your puppy will soon grow attached to a specific spot in the yard if you take her to the same place to do her business, every single time.

If your puppy has an accident indoors, be sure to use an odor neutralizer to fully rid the spot of any smells that send the "return here" signal to the puppy. I deal more with housebreaking in Chapter 7.

Chewing

Puppies chew. And your puppy hasn't learned yet what he should and shouldn't chew. Some breeds have a stronger chewing need than others. When your Boxer chews, you'll have a hard time missing it. Never underestimate the power of those Boxer jaws!

Don't leave your new pigskin gloves on the floor and then have a coronary because your dog ate them. Be kind enough to your puppy to avoid leaving temptation in his path, especially during teething time. A Chihuahua owner may return home to find their dog has left a tooth mark or two on the leg of the prized Chippendale table. But a Boxer owner will wonder where the whole leg disappeared to. A word to the wise: Bored Boxers are capable of renovating an entire household in a relatively short time. Either empty the room completely or, better yet, put your Boxer in his crate where he won't be tempted to demolish your antique collection while you are out.

Bitter Apple, Tabasco sauce, and other deterrents can help, but you can't drench your whole house in these products. Confinement with an enjoyable chew toy when you can't keep an eye on your pup is the wisest approach. And always have something the pup can chew on handy, even when you *are* home.

Energy bursts

I have always wondered what goes through a puppy's mind when she suddenly decides to take off on a mad dash through the house as though the devil himself was right on her tail. If nothing else, those gallops around the dining room table or through the halls are a way for the pup to burn up some of that excess energy that all puppies seem to have.

After your pup has one of those Indy 500 runs around the house, she'll probably immediately flop down and take a good long snooze. Nothing is wrong with your puppy if she does this. The only thing you have to watch out for is the puppy crashing into something and hurting herself. And, as her size increases, make sure the puppy doesn't crash into someone who could be hurt.

Make sure that your puppy doesn't attempt to snap at and grab at things as she goes running around the house; this behavior is definitely something that must be corrected immediately. You do not want to awaken a Boxer's desire to snatch at moving things. This can lead to chasing and biting at joggers and bicyclers.

Play biting and growling

Although a little tough-guy growling and chewing on your hand may be cute when your puppy is two or three months old, these habits are dangerous ones and shouldn't be encouraged. Growling and attempting to snatch things out of your hand gives a Boxer puppy the idea that this behavior is just fine anytime she wants to resort to it. It's your responsibility to make your Boxer understand that biting is never permissible — not even when it is done playfully. Stop the behavior before it becomes a problem. A Boxer must learn to relinquish anything he may be holding in his mouth or standing watch over when you command him to do so.

Separation anxiety

Separation anxiety is a far greater problem than most dog owners realize. This anxiety can be manifested in extremely destructive or neurotic behavior when the owner is absent. All too often, the behavior is dismissed as a simple temper tantrum done out of spite or done because the dog is just plain destructive. Animal shelter managers say that this problem, which can be dealt with effectively, is one of the major reasons that owners abandon their dogs or leave them to rescue organizations.

In most cases, behavior of this kind is due to the dog's uncontrollable fear of being left alone. The behavior is almost to be expected from dogs who have been abandoned at some point in their lives. Some dogs who have been forced to undergo an extreme change in their living conditions will also exhibit this neurotic and destructive behavior. Unwittingly, owners create or compound the problem by their own behavior. Don't add to your dog's insecurity by making your departure or return comparable to a soap opera cliffhanger. Going to the store is not *The Exodus,* so don't make it that. Just go. When you return, don't carry on like a reenactment of the return of the prodigal son. In fact, with a dog who is manifesting separation anxiety symptoms, you're better off completely ignoring the dog for 10 or 15 minutes after you do get back.

A drug called *Comicalm* can help to relieve separation anxiety so that gradual retraining can take place. The drug is actually an antidepressant or mood leveler that works in much the same way as its human counterpart, Prozac. If your Boxer is experiencing stress of this kind, discuss the problem with your veterinarian and see whether Comicalm is the right option for your dog.

Confine *all* dogs to a safe area while you are gone. This is especially important to do with a dog undergoing separation anxiety.

Being Prepared for Your Dog's Adolescence

The poor adolescent Boxer has a great deal to cope with just keeping those hormones from raging out of hand. On top of that, the pup is constantly switching back and forth between puppyhood and maturity, just like you did when you were a teenager. At this stage, your Boxer's guarding instinct also begins to develop and no one is less confident about what to do with it than the Boxer himself.

Guarding

At this stage of their lives, something deep stirs within your Boxer and tells her she should do something about the delivery man coming up to your front porch, but she isn't sure of just what that something is.

Usually, the budding guard dog will bark and then run off to hide. Another time your protector may beat a hasty retreat behind you and peek out between your legs barking furiously to let you know the two of you are in danger of losing life and limb. Your Boxer may know that the delivery man is a problem, but she's inexperienced, so she just isn't sure what the problem is or what to do about it.

If someone is going to be a frequent visitor to the premises, like your mail carrier, introduce the person to your dog and let them become familiar with each other.

Your Boxer *should* be wary and indicate the presence of someone they don't know and have never been introduced to.

Posting your yard or home with a sign saying, "guard dog on duty," may not be *entirely* true, but it's still entirely appropriate. Signs of this kind can be purchased at most hardware stores and pet stores. The booth merchants at dog shows often carry "Boxer on duty" placards that are very effective in warding off unwelcomed strangers. In many cases, these signs are posted even when there is no Boxer at home. Most would-be thieves are not particularly interested in testing the truth of such a warning.

Dominance

There are dominant and passive dogs in practically all breeds. With smaller dogs, dominance doesn't matter that much. But in larger dogs like Boxers, a dominant dog without direction can result in a dog who is the absolute antithesis of what was intended. This is where the proper owner and a well-devised training regimen are so important to a Boxer's achieving the level of stability and reliability it is capable of.

You and your human family are collectively your Boxer's pack leader. There must be no exceptions to this rule and, if enforced, your Boxer will always look to you and your family for guidance in all things.

A Boxer with any dominant inclinations who is pampered, whose every whim is catered to, begins to see himself as leader of the pack. Boxers who balk at giving up their playthings or who won't relinquish their spot on the sofa are looking to find their place in the order of things. You're responsible for letting your dog know where this is.

A pack leader does not arbitrate; a pack leader *demands*. There is no compromise when it comes to the rules. The members of the pack never have to wonder where their place is. If any member forgets his place or challenges the authority that dictated the order, the offender is quickly put back in line or ousted from the pack. Even when a challenger is victorious, authority is immediately reestablished and order is restored. There is no democracy in pack government, nor should there be in dog ownership.

Although kindness, respect, and tolerance must prevail in your relationship with your Boxer, there can never be a doubt (in your mind or your dog's) about who is in charge.

Pressure

All Boxers have similar characteristics, but they also have very distinct individual personalities. Some respond to a gentle reprimand; others don't seem to get the message unless three drill sergeants are shouting out the order. Each personality type requires an entirely different approach to training. A dominant male needs to be handled differently than a quiet, compliant little female. (I am only using these as examples, however. Not all males are bound to be bullies and not all females are little angels!).

The more passive pup is a lot more anxious to comply and will not need to be handled with the same kind of tough approach required for the extrovert. Bearing down too hard on a pup who was ready to comply in the first place can create a great deal of confusion and interfere with learning. The passive puppy's first reaction to a command could then be fright rather than enthusiasm about being given an opportunity to perform for you.

Too much training before a pup is ready or teaching a pup with too heavy a hand can upset some youngsters so much that they can become neurotic and destructive. Pay attention to what your individual dog actually needs. Just because you owned a dog that had to be run down by a bulldozer before the message got through doesn't mean that your new dog needs to be handled in the same way.

Chapter 7

Training Your New Dog

*B*oxers have a tremendous capacity to learn, but they can't learn unless they have committed owners who are willing to train them. And that's where *you* come in. Training takes a lot of patience and time, but if you view it as a way to bond with your dog, the process will be much more enjoyable for both of you. In this chapter, I cover everything from how dogs communicate to what you should do when you first bring your puppy home. If you're looking for tips on housebreaking, you'll find them in this chapter as well. And finally, I take you through the process of teaching your Boxer to obey specific commands. Whatever your training questions or concerns, you'll find valuable information in this chapter.

Understanding How to Communicate with Your Boxer

You and I are accustomed to learning about each other by listening to what the other person has to say. The more attention you give to someone speaking, and the more you dismiss your own preconceived notions and prejudices, the more apt you are to understand what the other person is really all about. Your relationship with your Boxer is based on exactly the same principle. Instead of listening with your ears, however, you have to learn to rely on an entirely different sense. After all, your Boxer can't communicate verbally. So you have to learn to interpret his behavior — because his behavior speaks as loudly as the words you or I use.

Dogs in the wild have communicated with each other through the use of growls, squeaks, and barks since the days when they were still wolves. Their major form of communication, however, is body language. Dogs listen to each other with their eyes and this is how you have to listen to your dog.

Recognizing active and passive behavior

The canine world's body language is a much simpler and far less ambiguous one than the spoken languages of humans. You can figure out a good part of a dog's body language very quickly by understanding two of a dog's basic attitudes: active and passive.

- **Active behavior:** Generally speaking, when a dog is exhibiting active behavior, he moves in a forward and up direction (whereas the passive dog will move backward and down). The challenging Boxer steps forward, stiff-legged, often with the hair on the back of his neck and shoulders standing up. The dog's head is up and he looks directly forward, staring at who or what is being challenged. A snarl emerges through clenched teeth. The tail is stiffened and carried in a semierect position. Everything about the dog's stance and attitude indicates that he plans to move ahead with whatever action he needs to take.

- **Passive behavior:** A dog usually indicates passive behavior by moving down and backward, folding up on himself. The passive dog's head is lowered and the ears are pinned back. If Boxers were dogs with long tails, they would hold their tails down and curled under their bodies.

Although you can learn a lot about your Boxer and what he's trying to tell you by determining whether he's exhibiting active or passive behavior, your Boxer's communication skills go far beyond these two basic types of behavior. You'll have much greater success in training and socializing your Boxer if you understand what he is trying to tell you. A Boxer seldom acts or reacts without giving some advance notice. Sometimes he may give this notice in very subtle ways, but if you make an effort to understand what these signals tell you, you'll be better prepared to anticipate your Boxer's response.

Dogs read anger very easily. Your Boxer may learn to dislike a command very quickly because you fly off the handle if she doesn't perform as soon as you think she should. Then she associates your anger with the lesson and anticipates that, immediately after you give the command, you'll be angry with her.

If you're having trouble getting your Boxer to obey your commands, pay close attention to the manner in which she refuses to obey. You'll begin to see that there is a difference in both expression and in body language between the dog who is ignoring your command and the dog who doesn't understand what you're asking for.

Making sense of the different theories on dog behavior

You and I obey laws because we are aware that swift and unpleasant consequences could result if we don't. We don't have to actually experience the consequences to know that they're there. We have the ability to conceptualize, to imagine what could happen to us if we break the law, and that's enough to keep most of us in line.

But in order for your dog to learn to obey the rules in your home, you have to understand how dogs operate. Dogs do it somewhat differently than humans do, and we can't approach them on the same terms that we would use in dealing with another human (at least not always).

If it sounds like I'm waffling, it's because I am. Some dog behaviorists tell us that all behavior shown by canines is purely instinctive, and they offer all kinds of proof to substantiate their belief. Other behaviorists insist that scientific studies prove otherwise, showing that dogs think. These two theories — instinctual theory and cognitive theory — are described below.

Instinctual theory

All dogs have some instinctive behaviors because they are, in fact, dogs. The wolves from whom all the dogs of the world have descended gave their descendants certain genes that have just hung in there through the ages. When humans recognized these hereditary inclinations, they manipulated the gene pools either to eradicate the characteristics or to cultivate them. In some instances, they just let them stand.

Purebred dogs have some instinctive behaviors peculiar to all dogs and some instinctive behaviors that are specific to the breed. You can't expect the Bulldog to have a burning desire to herd sheep, but you can count on the fact that certain breeds like the Australian Cattle Dog will. Cattle Dogs herd because this behavior has been passed down from wolf ancestors and has been selectively encouraged and refined. Granted, wolves had a much different purpose in mind when they herded, but man took care of that instinct by adding a pinch of reserve and a dash of trainability to suppress the need to dine on the animals they herded.

Eliminating a dog's breed-related behavior and responses is virtually impossible. For example, you can train a Border Collie not to chase after livestock, but that does not mean the dog will not have the *desire* to do so. Don't buy a breed of dog that is naturally inclined to behave in a certain manner and then expect it to react against that natural instinct.

Guarding and protective breeds, like our Boxers, aren't sent off to school to give them the desire to protect. They already have that desire instinctively. Boxers *are* given lessons, however, in how to control and channel those protective instincts in a manner that will be both suitable and beneficial to their owners.

Cognitive theory

The only people I know who are willing to say that dogs don't think things out and come up with a logical conclusion have never lived with the same dog for any length of time. When your Boxer starts hunting up her leash to let you know she's decided it's time for a stroll or when she stands between your child and the street and refuses to budge, you may question a dog's purported inability to think or reason.

But just because dogs may be able to think or reason to some degree doesn't mean that they always use the good sense they have. (After all, humans don't, and we're supposed to be fully rational beings!). Dogs are inclined to be as wise as Methuselah at one time and absolutely witless at another. Don't expect your Boxer not to run off and romance the girl dog across the street just because the 5:00 rush hour is on. Left to his own devices, the drive that takes your dog across the street will outweigh any love he has for you. His wolf nature tells him that visiting his true love is the thing to do. Unless he has learned there are consequences to breaking your rules, your Boxer will follow his instincts.

Reinforcing the Behavior You Want and Discouraging the Behavior You Don't

Your Boxer learns to avoid breaking a specific rule because every time she breaks that particular rule she experiences something unpleasant — a snap of the leash or a harsh tone of voice from you, for example. Breaking the rules results in this unpleasant experience. In order to associate the unpleasant experience with the act, the unpleasant experience must occur immediately after the dog has broken the rules.

This unpleasant experience must happen *every* time a certain behavior occurs — not *some* of the time but *all* of the time.

Humans usually do the right thing because we have been lead to believe that "good" people do it this way and "bad" people do it the other way. We understand the concepts of *good* and *bad*. We don't need a piece of candy to encourage us to eat our veggies. We eat them because they are good for us. Your Boxer, on the other hand, is a sucker for bribery. When he barks on command, he gets a doggie treat. And he quickly learns that barking brings a treat. On the other hand, your Boxer may learn that she can't bark her head off any time she wants, because that behavior leads to a rebuke or a squirt in the face rather than a treat or a pat on the head.

So if dogs learn to associate rewards (like treats) with good behavior and punishment (like a squirt of water in the face) with bad behavior, why do they insist upon doing things that will get them in trouble? Your Boxer knows she will get into trouble when she empties the trash can and scatters its contents all over the kitchen, but she keeps doing it. Evidently, she gets some reward (a pork chop perhaps?) when she empties the trash. Now, what is worse in your dog's mind — you being upset or the dog missing out on those gourmet treats she finds in the trash? She may hate the scolding, but her burning desire for those delectable morsels is satisfied when she raids the trash can. After several successful trash can raids, she knows for certain there is a pot of gold at the end of that rainbow! She's forgotten about the scolding, because that comes later. The pork chop comes now — and that's all she's thinking about.

Ideally, your Boxer should not have been allowed to get into the trash can the first time. When she was able to do it again the second and third time, she became satisfied that the thrill of victory was worth the agony of getting caught!

Every time your Boxer repeats an undesirable act, the more difficult it is to remove that behavior from the dog's memory.

Knowing why your Boxer breaks the rules is one thing, but that doesn't make her spreading the contents of the trashcan all over the house any more acceptable.

Sometimes punishment is the right response, but the punishment itself must be appropriate. Some things your Boxer does will be mildly upsetting; other things may make you furious. Never make the mistake, however, of interpreting your dog's actions in human terms. Vengeance and retaliation are human characteristics. What you may interpret as retaliation on the part of your dog is far more likely to be instinct or even anxiety and frustration. Although it may seem like it, your Boxer did *not* diabolically plan to get back at you.

Assuming your Boxer has intentionally done something to spite you is a foolish error in judgment on your part. Flying off into a rage because of the behavior is both unfair and dangerous. Unfair, because dogs are not vengeful creatures, and dangerous, because a Boxer is not a breed whose history makes it willing to accept that kind of treatment. There is a vast difference between punishment for an infraction of rules and abuse.

If your Boxer misbehaves, you need to respond to the dog by being calm, fair, and consistent. If you are unable to interact with a Boxer on that basis, day in and day out, you most certainly should not be a dog owner.

Knowing Your Role in Your Boxer's Life

As a Boxer puppy leaves the nest, she begins to search for two things: a pack leader and the rules set down by that leader. The mentally sound Boxer mother fulfills both of these needs unhesitatingly. However, new puppy owners often fail miserably in supplying these very basic needs. Instead, owners usually begin to respond to the demands of the puppy — and Boxer puppies can quickly learn to be very demanding.

If your young puppy cannot find her pack leader in you, she will assume those duties herself. If you impose no rules, the clever little Boxer puppy quickly learns to make the kinds of rules she likes. The longer this scenario goes on, the more difficult it will be to change.

Boxers are extremely sensitive. A whack on the butt or a good loud reprimand barely made a dent on the Sporting Dogs I've owned and have meant absolutely nothing to my Bull Terriers. But Boxers are an entirely different story. With Boxers, by and large, positive reinforcement is the key to success, and it produces a happy and confident companion. Your Boxer puppy should always be a winner. Begin teaching simple lessons like the *come* command when the puppy is already on her way to you. Be reasonable however. Don't expect the just-learning young puppy to come dashing over to you when she is engrossed in some wonderful adventure. And never allow your puppy to associate the *come* command with anger or punishment.

Figuring Out Which Lessons to Start With

When your puppy first arrives home, you may be overwhelmed by all the lessons you have to teach him. Or you may be so wrapped up in how cute he is that you forget all about training. In this section, I cover some basics that you can teach your puppy right away, without working too hard.

Socialization

Right on the heels of your Boxer's need for food and water comes a need for early and continual socialization. If there is one lesson that all dogs must learn, it is to get along well with humans. Your dog doesn't have to love every stranger that crosses his path, but he has to understand that humans lay down the rules and regulations and that he must learn to abide by them without hesitation.

Temperament is both hereditary and learned. Inherited good temperament can be ruined by poor treatment and lack of socialization. A Boxer puppy who has inherited a bad temperament is dangerous as a companion or as a show dog and should certainly never be bred. Obtaining a happy, well-adjusted puppy from a breeder who is determined to produce good temperaments and has taken all the necessary steps to provide the early socialization necessary is critical.

Just because the puppies in a given litter are the result of good care, however, does not mean that socialization and temperament are a finished product. The responsible Boxer breeder begins the socialization process as soon as the puppies enter the world. Constant handling, exposure to strange sights and sounds, weighing, and nail trimming are all experiences that help the growing Boxer understand that this is a human's world and that she is entirely safe and secure when she is with human beings. The puppy is learning that, after her mother, the best care and comfort comes from people.

Households with dog-wise children are a fantastic environment for puppies to spend the first several weeks of their lives. Puppies and children have a natural affinity for each other, and those children who are well trained in puppy care and sufficiently supervised have no equal in the socialization department. Children seem able to teach puppies things like eating from their own dish and behaving for cleanup with relative ease. They have a knack of breaking up puppy squabbles, and it seems to take children minutes to leash-train a puppy, even though the same pup will balk and refuse when an adult tries the same thing.

We have friends who come to visit with their young daughter, who brings a whole wardrobe of doll clothes to dress our puppies in. The puppies even have the opportunity to get rides in the doll carriage. They adore all the attention and go to their new homes thinking that children are the greatest playmates in the world.

Secluded sheltered puppies who never see a stranger until they are ready to go off to their new homes are a poor risk in the temperament department. Their ability to take strangers and strange situations in stride lacks cultivation. With reasonable care, after the puppies have had their first inoculations, they should be given the benefit of as many strange sights, sounds, and people as possible. Responsible breeders also make it a point to introduce their puppies to strange environments — if the gang has been raised in the kitchen, for example, a trip outdoors. The breeder may also give one puppy at a time special attention in the family room, as a way of socializing each dog individually, away from his littermates.

At this early stage, puppies are becoming accustomed to different tones of voice and voice inflections. It is never too early for a puppy to learn the meaning of "no." As long as it's not followed by punishment of any kind, gently guiding a puppy away from danger with a firm "no" tells a pup that there are rules and that you're the one enforcing them.

The socialization must continue when the puppy arrives at your home as well. In fact, socialization must continue through the rest of the dog's life with you. You don't want the entire neighborhood waiting with a drum and bugle corps when the pup first arrives home, but increase the new sights, sounds, and people with each passing day. A Boxer puppy may be as happy as a clam living at home with you and your family, but if you don't continue the socialization begun by the breeder, that sunny disposition will not extend outside your front door.

From the day the young Boxer arrives at your home, you must be committed to helping the puppy meet and coexist with all human beings and animals. Never encourage aggressive behavior on the part of your puppy. And don't encourage your pup to fear strangers.

Take your puppy everywhere with you — the post office, along busy streets, to the shopping mall. Be prepared to create a stir wherever you go. The public seems to hold a special admiration for the Boxer, and although they may not want to approach a mature dog, most people are quite taken with the Boxer baby and will undoubtedly want to pet your youngster. There is nothing in the world better for the puppy than friendly strangers! Carry treats with you when you go out. If your puppy backs off from a stranger, give the person one of the little snacks and have that person offer it to your puppy. Insist your young Boxer be amenable to the attention of any strangers you approve of, regardless of sex, age, or race. Your puppy doesn't get to decide who he will or will not tolerate. You are in charge, and you must call the shots.

Do not make the mistake of thinking that you should isolate your pup in order to ensure the Boxer's guarding or protective abilities. Meeting everyone in town with a wagging tail will have no affect whatsoever on the territorial character of the adult Boxer. The maturing Boxer will definitely know what is yours and will be as devoted as you are in preserving it.

All Boxers must learn to get on with other dogs as well as with humans. If you are fortunate enough to have a puppy preschool or dog training class nearby, attend with as much regularity as you possibly can. A young Boxer who has been exposed regularly to other dogs from puppyhood will learn to adapt and accept other dogs and other breeds much more readily than one who seldom ever sees strange dogs. Check out the section "Enrolling Your Pup in School" for more information on training classes and where to find a good trainer.

If you have other animals, your Boxer puppy will be meeting with and interacting with them for the first time. Previous occupants deserve seniority treatment. Don't confine the pets who have already established residence. (The puppy is the one who is invading their territory.) Instead, confine the puppy to an area of the house where the other animals won't feel the need to frequent. Let the previous residents check out the pup at their leisure and at the pace they choose. Eventually, your Boxer and your other animals will at the very least get along. And they may even become the best of friends (see Figure 7-1).

Figure 7-1:
This Boxer is checking out the kitten who shares his home. Be sure to always allow your animals time and distance when introducing them to one another.

Photograph by Phyllis Shaffer

Name recognition

Decide on a name for your puppy before you bring the little guy home. Your dog's name is one of the first things she should become familiar with. Name recognition is the puppy's first step in identifying with her new home. Notice that after just a couple of days of hearing that familiar word, the pup will respond by wagging her little tail and giving you that, "You mean me?" kind of look.

Use your pup's name as often as you can. Preface everything you say to your puppy with the puppy's name.

Proper puppy behavior

After the initial day or so of unfamiliarity, your Boxer pup will begin to regain his confidence and start showing you a complete repertoire of antics that only puppies and kittens are capable of. Unfortunately, as cute as some of these little behaviors are, many of them have to be curbed. Play biting, chewing, jumping up, dragging the sofa pillows off into the next room — all of those things that are too cute for words now will not be things you'll appreciate in your adult Boxer. You have to harden your heart, be a killjoy, and nip bad habits in the bud. Look at it this way: Stopping your pup from these typical puppy antics will actually be teaching him the first two very important lifelong lessons — name recognition and the meaning of the word *no*.

No

One of the most important kindergarten lessons your Boxer puppy will ever learn is the meaning of *no*. No is the one command the puppy can begin learning the minute he first arrives in your home. You don't have to frighten your puppy into learning the meaning of *no*, but you should never give this or any other command you are not prepared and able to enforce. The only way a puppy learns to obey commands is to realize that when they're issued, commands must be complied with.

Use the *no* command just as soon as your Boxer pup grabs the end of the table-cloth or eyeballs the electric plug on the wall. Screaming "no" after the damage is done does nothing at all to further her education. Dogs do not associate a reprimand with something they've done in the past. In fact, reprimands after the fact will probably serve to confuse your Boxer rather than teach her you do not approve. If you pay enough attention to your pup, you'll be able to "hear" her say, "I think I'll eat that potted palm now," by her body language. And you can stop it before it starts.

Leash-training

Getting your Boxer puppy used to her leash and collar can never come too soon. The leash and collar are your fail-safe way of keeping your dog under control. It may not be necessary for the puppy or adult Boxer to wear her collar and identification tags within the confines of her own home, but no dog should ever be outdoors in an unsecured area without a collar around her neck and the leash held securely in your hand.

Begin getting your puppy accustomed to this new experience by leaving a soft collar around her neck for a few minutes at a time. Gradually extend the time you leave the collar on. Most Boxer puppies become accustomed to their collars very quickly and after a few scratches to remove it, forget they are even wearing one. While you are playing with the puppy, attach a lightweight leash to the collar. Do not try to guide the puppy at first. The point here is to accustom the puppy to the feeling of having something hanging from the collar.

At first, follow the puppy while you hold the leash. After a bit, try to encourage the puppy to follow you as you move away. If the puppy is reluctant to cooperate, coax her along with a treat of some kind. Hold the treat in front of the puppy's nose to encourage her to follow you. Just as soon as the puppy takes a few steps toward you, praise her enthusiastically, giving the pup a tiny bit of the treat and continuing to do so as you move slowly along.

Make the initial sessions short and fun. Continue the lessons in your home or yard until the puppy is completely unconcerned with the fact that she is on a leash. With a treat in one hand and the leash in the other, you can begin to use both to guide the puppy in the direction you want to go. Begin your first walks in front of the house and eventually extend them down the street and then around the block. Try to encourage the pup to walk on your left side; this will come in handy later when you try to train more complicated behaviors.

Housebreaking 101: Your Guide to Getting It Done Right

Boxers generally are very easy to housebreak, because the breed is an exceptionally clean one. However, if you are inconsistent or lackadaisical in your approach to housebreaking, your Boxer will get a mixed message and, as a result, may well decide to do what has to be done wherever he wants.

The method of housebreaking I recommend is avoidance. The task of housebreaking gets progressively harder each time a puppy is allowed to have an accident indoors. Take your puppy outdoors to relieve himself after every meal, after every nap, and after every 15 or 20 minutes of playtime. Carry the puppy outdoors to avoid the opportunity of an accident occurring on the way out.

Housebreaking your Boxer becomes a much easier task with the use of a crate. Begin feeding your Boxer puppy in the crate. Keep the door closed and latched while the puppy is eating. When the meal is finished, open the cage and carry the puppy outdoors to the spot where you want the pup to learn to eliminate. If you don't have outdoor access or if you will be away from home for long periods of time, begin housebreaking by placing newspapers in some out-of-the-way corner that is easily accessible for the puppy. If you consistently take your puppy to the same spot, you will reinforce the habit of going there for that purpose.

Do not let the puppy loose after eating. Young puppies eliminate almost immediately after eating or drinking. They are also ready to relieve themselves when they first wake up and after playing. If you keep a watchful eye on your puppy, you will quickly learn when this is about to happen. A puppy usually circles and sniffs the floor just before he relieves himself. Do not give your puppy an opportunity to learn that he can eliminate in the house! Your housebreaking chores will be reduced considerably if you avoid bad habits beginning in the first place.

If you are not able to watch your puppy every minute, he should be in his cage or crate with the door securely latched. Each time you put your puppy in the crate, give him a small treat of some kind. Throw the treat to the back of the cage and encourage the puppy to walk in on his own. When he does so, praise the puppy and perhaps hand him another piece of the treat through the wires of the cage.

A Boxer puppy of eight to twelve weeks will not be able to contain himself for long periods of time. Puppies of that age must relieve themselves often, except at night. Your schedule must be adjusted accordingly. Also, make sure your puppy has relieved himself at night before the last member of the family goes to bed.

In the morning, your first priority is to get the puppy outdoors. Just how early this needs to happen depends much more upon your puppy than upon you. If your Boxer is like most others, you'll have no doubt when he needs to be let out. You'll also learn very quickly to tell the difference between the puppy's "emergency" signals and just unhappy grumbling. Don't test the young puppy's ability to contain himself. His early-morning vocal demand to be let out is confirmation that the housebreaking lesson is being learned.

If you have to be away from home all day, don't leave your puppy in a crate. But don't make the mistake of allowing him to roam the house or even a large room at will either. Confine the puppy to a small room or partitioned-off area, and cover the floor with newspaper. Make this area large enough so that the puppy does not have to relieve himself next to his bed, food, or water bowls. The puppy will soon be inclined to use one particular spot to perform his bowel and bladder functions. When you are home, you must take the puppy to this exact spot to eliminate at the appropriate time. That way, you'll encourage the pup to use the same spot every time.

Basic Training

Puppy boot camp begins on the day the pup arrives home. And guess who the drill sergeant is? That's right — it's you! Keep in mind a few things that will help you accomplish all the goals you've set for your little trainee.

First, there is no breed of dog that cannot be trained. Some breeds provide a real challenge to training, but in most cases this has more to do with trainers and their training methods than with any dog's inability to learn.

Using the proper approach, any dog who is not mentally deficient can be taught to be a good canine citizen. Many dog owners do not understand how a dog learns, nor do they realize they can and should be breed-specific in their approach to training.

If you own a Boxer, you should be aiming for some basic behavior minimums from the first day your puppy enters your home. The rewards of owning this great breed are practically limitless, but to gain access to what has earned Boxers their great reputation, you must provide the framework from which your dog will reliably operate. The following is a checklist that all Boxer owners should consider a basic part of their dog's education:

- ✔ Walk on a leash quietly at your side, even on a crowded street.
- ✔ Allow any stranger to pet him when you give the signal that it's okay.
- ✔ Come immediately when called.
- ✔ Sit and lie down on command and remain in position until you give the *come* command.
- ✔ Be tolerant of other dogs and pets.

These behaviors are ones that every companion Boxer should be taught. Your Boxer is more than capable of mastering all of these behaviors, and it is up to you to make sure he or she is given the opportunity to do so.

Boxers are not only highly capable of learning, they thrive on training, especially if it appears to be a fun game. Even young Boxer puppies have an amazing capacity to learn. This capacity is greater than most humans realize. Keep in mind, however, that these young puppies also forget with great speed, unless they are reminded of what they have learned by continual reinforcement.

Come

One of the most important lessons for the Boxer puppy to learn is to come when called. Learning to come on command could save your Boxer's life when the two of you venture out into the world. *Come* is the command a dog must understand has to be obeyed without question, but the dog should not associate that command with fear. Your dog's response to her name and the word *come* should always be associated with a pleasant experience, such as great praise and petting or a food treat.

All too often, novice trainers get very angry at their dog for not responding immediately to the *come* command. When the dog finally does come or after the owner has chased the dog down, the owner scolds the dog for not obeying. The dog begins to associate *come* with an unpleasant result. Again, avoiding the establishment of bad habits is much easier than correcting them after they've set in. Avoid at all costs giving the *come* command unless you are sure your puppy will come to you. The very young Boxer puppy is far more inclined to respond to learning the *come* command than the older dog who has never been introduced to the word. Use the command initially when the puppy is already on her way to you, or give the command while walking or running away from the youngster. Clap your hands and sound very happy and excited about having the puppy join in on this game.

Later, as a puppy grows more self-confident and independent, you may want to attach a long leash or rope to the puppy's collar to ensure the correct response. Again, do not chase or punish your puppy for not obeying the *come* command. Doing so in the initial stages of training makes the youngster associate the command with something to fear, and this will result in avoidance rather than the immediate positive response you desire. Always praise your puppy and give her a treat when she does come to you, even if she voluntarily delays responding for many minutes.

Sit and stay

Just as important to your Boxer's safety (and your sanity!) as the *no* command and learning to come when called are the *sit* and *stay* commands. Most Boxer puppies learn the *sit* command easily, often in just a few minutes, especially if it appears to be a game and a doggie treat is involved.

Your puppy should always be on collar and leash for his lessons. Young puppies are not beyond getting up and walking away when they have decided you and your lessons are boring.

Give the *sit* command (being sure to use your dog's name, too) immediately before pushing down on your pup's hindquarters or scooping his hind legs under him and molding him into a sit position. Praise your puppy lavishly when he does sit, even though you're the one who made the action take place. A food treat always seems to get the lesson across to the learning youngster.

Continue holding the dog's rear end down and repeat the *sit* command several times. If your dog makes an attempt to get up, repeat the command yet again, while exerting pressure on your dog's rear end until the correct position is assumed. Make your Boxer stay in this position for increasing lengths of time. Begin with a few seconds and increase the time as lessons progress over the following weeks.

If your young student attempts to get up or to lie down, correct him by simply repeating, "sit," in a firm voice, and return him to the desired position.

Only when you decide your dog can get up should he be allowed to do so. Do not test a very young puppy's patience to the limits. As brilliant as the Boxer puppy is, remember you are dealing with a baby. The attention span of any youngster, whether canine or human, is relatively short. When you do decide your puppy can get up, call his name, say "Roscoe, okay," and make a big fuss over him. Praise and a food treat are in order every time your puppy responds correctly. Continue to help your puppy assume proper positions or respond to commands until he performs on his own. This way your puppy always wins — he gets it right every time. This is training with positive reinforcement.

Long sit

When your Boxer has mastered the *sit* lesson, you can start working on the *stay* command. With your dog on her leash and at your left side, give the *sit* command. Put the palm of your right hand in front of your dog's eyes and say, "Stay." Take a small step forward. If she attempts to get up to follow you, firmly say, "Sit, stay." While you are saying this, raise your hand, palm toward her, and again command, "Stay."

Any attempt on your Boxer's part to get up must be corrected at once, returning her to the sit position, holding your palm up, and repeating, "Stay." When your Boxer begins to understand what you want, you can gradually increase the distance you step back. With a long leash attached to your dog's collar, start with a few steps and gradually increase the distance to several yards. Your Boxer must eventually learn that the *sit* and *stay* commands must be obeyed no matter how far away you are. Later on, with advanced training, your dog will learn the command should be obeyed even when you move entirely out of sight.

As your Boxer masters this lesson and is able to remain in the sit position for as long as you dictate, avoid calling your dog to you at first. Calling your dog makes her overly anxious to get up and run to you. Instead, walk back to your dog and say "Okay," which is a signal that the command is over. Later, when your Boxer becomes more reliable in this respect, you can call her to you.

Keep the *stay* part of the lesson to a minimum until your puppy is at least five or six months old. Everything in a very young Boxer's makeup urges her to stay close to you wherever you go. The puppy has bonded to you and forcing her to operate against her natural instincts can be bewildering. The important thing here is to teach the puppy that your command is to be obeyed until and unless you give a different command.

Down

When your Boxer has mastered the *sit* and *stay* commands, you can begin working on *down*. Down is the one-word command for "lie down." Use the *down* command only when you want the dog to lie down. If you want your dog to get off your sofa or to stop jumping up on people use the *off* command. Don't interchange the two commands. Doing so only serves to confuse your dog and will delay the response you want.

The down position is especially useful if you want your Boxer to remain in a particular place for an extended period of time. A dog is usually far more inclined to stay put when he is lying down than when he is sitting.

Teaching the down command to some Boxers may take a little more time and patience. The down position represents submissiveness to a dog. So the more forceful breeds and the dogs within those breeds who are inclined to be more dominant may take more time to develop any enthusiasm for this exercise.

With your Boxer sitting in front of and facing you, hold a treat in your right hand with the excess part of the leash in your left hand. Hold the treat under the dog's nose and slowly bring your hand down to the ground. Your dog will follow the treat with his head and neck. As he does, give the command "Down," and exert light pressure on his shoulders with your left hand. If he resists the pressure, do not continue pushing down, because doing so will only create more resistance.

An alternative method of getting your Boxer headed into the down position is to move around to the dog's right side and, as you draw his attention downward with your right hand, slide your left arm under the dog's front legs and gently slide them forward. In the case of a small puppy, you will undoubtedly have to be on your knees next to the youngster to do this.

As your Boxer's forelegs begin to slide out to his front, keep moving the treat along the ground until his whole body is lying on the ground while you continually repeat "Down." After he has assumed the position you desire, give him the treat and a lot of praise. Continue assisting him into the down position until he does so on his own. Be firm and be patient.

You can teach your Boxer the *long down* following the same basic procedure you use in working on the *long sit.* With your dog on a leash and at your left side, give the *down* command. Put the palm of your right hand in front of your dog's eyes and say "Stay!" Take a small step forward. If she attempts to get up to follow you, firmly say, "Down," and then, "Stay!" While you are saying this, raise your hand, with your palm toward the dog, and again command, "Stay!"

When your Boxer begins to understand what you want, you can gradually increase the distance you step back. Use a long leash and start with a few steps back, gradually increasing the distance to several yards.

Walking on a loose lead

Walking on a loose lead is important for two reasons. First, it is difficult enough to walk a Boxer *puppy* who is attempting to pull your arm out of its socket. But when your Boxer is fully grown, you are going to find yourself in a horizontal position, hanging onto the lead as he races down the street with you streaming behind.

I have found the link training collar very useful for leash lessons. It provides both quick pressure around the neck and a snapping sound, both of which get the dog's attention. Some people refer to this as a *choke collar*. But when it's used properly, it does *not* choke a dog. The pet store from which you purchase the collar will be able to show you the proper way to put this collar on your dog.

Do not leave a choke collar on your puppy when training sessions are finished. Because the collars fit loosely, they can get hooked on protruding objects and cause injury or even death. Also, when you use this collar, your Boxer knows that it's time to get down to business, not just a casual saunter.

As you train your puppy to walk on a leash, you should insist that the youngster walk on your left side. The leash crosses your body from the dog's collar to your right hand. The excess portion of the leash folds into your right hand and your left hand is then free on the leash to make corrections. Keep the leash slack and only tighten it to give a quick jerk to get your dog back in position. A quick short jerk on the leash with your left hand will keep your dog from lunging side to side, pulling ahead, or lagging back. As you make a correction, give the *heel* command with the dog's name. Keep the leash slack as long as your dog maintains the proper position at your side. Insisting that your Boxer walks quietly along with no pressure or strain on the leash will avoid giving the dog the urge to pull you along. If your dog begins to drift away, give the leash a sharp jerk and guide the dog back to the left side. Do not pull on the lead with steady pressure. Instead, give a sharp jerking motion to get your dog's attention. Eventually, your pup will automatically go to your left side as you walk.

Heel

In learning to heel, your Boxer will walk on your left side with his shoulder next to your leg no matter which direction you go or how quickly you turn. Your fingers should be able to touch your dog's shoulder, with your left arm hanging directly down at your left side. If you have to swing your arm out or bend your fingers, the dog is not in the right position.

The dog should not lag behind, move on ahead of you, or drift away from your side. Insisting on heeling in a precise way is very important when the two of you are out walking in public places. A Boxer who obeys this command properly will make a far more tractable companion when the two of you are in crowded or confusing situations. If you plan to progress on to formal obedience training, this is one of the lessons that all trainers will demand your dog follows without fail.

Begin with your Boxer sitting at your left side with his shoulder next to your leg. Step forward on your right foot and, as you step forward, give the *heel* command. The leash should be slack. After you start off, your dog will probably move out with you. If he attempts to pull away in any direction, give the sharp jerk and command him to heel. Do not keep the leash taut and attempt to pull the dog back into position. The well-trained Boxer will maintain the correct position no matter how fast or slow you go and no matter which direction you turn, including your doing an abrupt about-face.

You should always make corrections with a sharp jerk — with one exception. Occasionally a dog may be frightened or intimidated by the exercise. In this case, do not administer the jerk. Coax the dog into position and try to make obeying a fun game and worthy of a treat when done well. If the dog is still extremely intimidated, you can purchase cloth training collars, which may make your dog feel better (although they don't work as well).

Enrolling Your Pup in School

You can do a lot of training on your own, but sometimes enrolling in a class with your dog can be a good way of going that extra step. Training classes also add structure to your training, and you may see faster results — if only because you're forced to train your dog for a specified amount of time every week.

Training classes

There are few limits to what a patient, consistent owner can teach his or her Boxer. For advanced basic obedience, which all Boxers should have, and for work beyond that, consider local professional assistance. Qualified professional trainers have had long-standing experience in avoiding the pitfalls of obedience training and can help you to avoid these mistakes as well. Even Boxer owners who have never trained a dog before have found, with professional assistance, that their dog has become a superstar in obedience circles.

Training assistance can be obtained in many ways. Classes are particularly important for your Boxer's socialization and concentration. Most Boxers look at every new dog and every person they haven't met, as potential playmates. But at the same time, Boxers deal with these meetings with such exuberance that they are often off in their own little world. Your Boxer needs to learn to respond regardless of the surrounding conditions, and training classes are a great place for him to learn this.

Free-of-charge classes are offered at many parks and recreation facilities. Very formal and sometimes very expensive individual lessons with private trainers are also available in most cities. Some obedience schools take your Boxer for a period of time and train the dog for you. A Boxer can and will learn with any good professional. However, unless your schedule gives you no time at all to train your own dog, having someone else train the dog for you is not a good option. The rapport that develops between a Boxer and an owner who has trained the dog to be a pleasant companion and good canine citizen is very special — well worth the time and patience it requires to achieve.

Finding a good trainer

When you decide to seek the help of a dog trainer, you will probably be overwhelmed by the number of them available. All trainers will claim to have years of experience and be capable of using a training method previously unknown to mankind but guaranteed to make your dog a canine *Jeopardy!* candidate and a shoo-in for a costarring role in the next *Lassie* film. Take promises of overnight success with a grain of salt. Smart as our Boxers are, good trainers take as much time with each dog as is necessary, and no two dogs absorb the training at the same rate of speed. Good dog training is about training your dog well, not how fast the dog completes the course.

Don't misunderstand what a dog trainer's real purpose is. The ideal trainer is one who is experienced at teaching *you* to train your dog. The fact that an outsider is able to have your Boxer behave like a perfect lady will have no affect upon her behavior at home if you are not equipped to enforce the rules.

Here are some tips for finding a trainer who will be able to teach you and your Boxer what you both need to know — in a manner that is suitable for the breed:

- ✔ Always check to see how long the trainer has been in business and whether he or she has references that you can contact. (And be sure to contact those references if they're available.)

- ✔ The trainer should have a working knowledge of many breeds with a good understanding of their origin, purpose, and differences. The trainer should definitely have an awareness of the different instinctual behaviors found in the different breeds of dogs, particularly Boxers.

- ✔ The trainer should have had prior experience in training Boxers.

- ✔ Be wary of a trainer who promises overnight perfection or makes claims that sound too good to be true.

- ✔ Good professional trainers always put what they intend to teach your dog in writing and will always offer post-training assistance if you experience problems.

- ✔ If there are specific things you don't want your dog taught or if there are training methods you object to, make your wishes clear to the trainer. The trainer's methods or goals may be in conflict with yours.

> ✔ The trainer should be able to explain to you what is required in the various levels of obedience training as well as what is required for specialized training (such as agility) and the super-advanced obedience levels.
>
> ✔ Professional trainers have a standard rate list so that you will know beforehand just how much your dog's education will cost you.
>
> ✔ Although many trainers have proven extremely capable of training Boxers, there is no substitute for trainers who have bred and raised the breed themselves.

Experienced professionals have no objection to discussing any of the items on this list. They have the knowledge to back up their answers and do not feel threatened by your questions. Be very leery of any trainer who is unable or reluctant to answer the questions you pose.

Dealing with Emotional Conflicts

It's virtually impossible for two animals (human or otherwise) to participate in a relationship without occasional conflict. But when emotions constantly run at a high pitch, problems do arise both for us humans and for the dogs who live in our homes.

Dogs can be extremely sensitive to discord within the human family. The conflicts that remain unresolved and fester just below the surface over long periods of time are particularly damaging to a dog's emotional stability. Dogs see the conflict as part of their concern, and they aren't capable of knowing who is right or who is wrong. They feel, for lack of a better word, the hostility. As the conflict lingers the dog's state of unrest continues until it begins to manifest itself in poor behavior, in poor health, or in both.

Husband-wife conflicts or exceedingly hostile sibling rivalry probably won't resolve themselves because the tension is causing problems for the family dog. Still, considering the possibility that an unstable environment is causing your dog's bad behavior may work in the dog's behalf. Rehoming your dog into a more suitable situation could give the dog and another family an opportunity for an enjoyable relationship. Particularly sensitive breeds are highly susceptible to environmental conditions. When I say *sensitive,* I do not necessarily mean shy or fragile dogs. I believe that the more intelligent breeds are especially attuned to their owners' feelings and are at greatest risk in this area. I include the Boxer among this group of sensitive dogs. Boxers are highly intelligent, extremely devoted, and very territorial — all factors contributing to a high sensitivity level.

Those of us who admire the Boxer are fully aware that the breed's over-the-top personality, when unchecked, can be a distinct nuisance rather than the asset it was intended to be. A high energy level, friendliness, and determination are the components that help create the free-spirited character that is another admirable trait of the breed. However, when your Boxer is consistently allowed to do what he wants to do, and only when he wants to do it, he may have great difficulty in harnessing his energy and bending to the rules when you find it necessary to impose them.

Boxers who have had no restraints growing up can respond to having their reins tightened with some highly unacceptable behavior. An inability to focus, stubbornness, and often outright rebellion are not uncommon reactions. Behavior of this kind is undesirable in any dog but inexcusable in a dog the size of a Boxer.

Although we cannot be permissive in dealing with a Boxer, neither can we be overbearing. A dog with the strength of character that a well-bred Boxer normally possesses must be given direction, but you cannot constantly browbeat and harass a Boxer without ill effects. Hitting your Boxer or frenzied yelling at every minor infraction will only serve to create a dog who lives in constant confusion and fear. A dog like this has no safe haven and being forced into any new or distasteful situation can create panic.

If your Boxer is acting and reacting in a socially unacceptable manner, the cause may or may not be the way in which you have been approaching the dog's training and discipline. Regardless of whether the mistake is yours, you must seek professional help to help you and your dog get back on track at once.

Where should you go for help? If you haven't remained in touch with the breeder from whom you bought your Boxer, this is time to correct that situation. The minute you suspect any behavior problem, your breeder is the first person you should speak to. An experienced breeder will undoubtedly be able to suggest someone who would be most able to help you through your problem situation.

The proper solution may be a trainer experienced in dealing with problem dogs or possibly an animal behaviorist. You and you alone are responsible for the behavior of your Boxer, and it is up to you to find the most suitable solution to any behavior problems that develop. There are invariably causes and cures to problems of this kind — but they may be beyond your realm of experience.

Part IV
Maintaining Your Boxer's Health

Shoot, that ain't nothin', watch this—Roll over, Rusty. C'mon, roll over! Roll over!

In this part . . .

The chapters in this part cover everything from feeding and grooming your Boxer to taking care of him when he gets sick. In this part, you'll figure out how to prevent health problems from starting, and you'll get useful information on recognizing and dealing with them if they affect your Boxer. You'll also find great tips for avoiding emergencies and dealing with them if and when they come up. If you're looking for information on any facet of your Boxer's health, you've come to the right part.

Chapter 8

Getting to Know Your Boxer . . . Inside and Out

*A*s an owner of a Boxer, you need to be as familiar with your Boxer as you are with yourself. So in this chapter, I give you all the information you need on your Boxer's anatomy. When you read the first part in this chapter, you'll be able to tell the difference between the stifle and the hock — and impress your vet with your knowledge. I also let you know what kinds of health problems your Boxer may encounter over the course of his lifetime so you can know what to look for.

In this chapter, you also get advice on whether you should breed your Boxer and what kinds of alterations (like tail docking and ear cropping) you'll want to consider. Finally, I end with perhaps the most important information of all: how to find and work with a good veterinarian, someone who will grow to be a great friend to both you and your Boxer.

The Anatomy of the Boxer

Understanding how your Boxer is put together is more than just some good information to have in mind for your next game of Trivial Pursuit. If you're familiar with your dog's anatomy, you'll be able to more clearly convey to your veterinarian any problems that your dog is having. You'll feel better being able to use precise terminology than having to vaguely describe where you think the problem may be.

Healthy, wealthy, and wise

The well-bred and well-raised Boxer is basically a very healthy dog with a love of humans and an extroverted personality that is the envy of owners of many other breeds. Sick dogs are not only an unhappy situation, they cost a good amount of money to cure. If you don't believe me, just ask your veterinarian.

You and your well-bred Boxer will share a relatively carefree life together if you give your pal reasonable care and lots of training and affection. With that all-important preventive maintenance, you won't have to worry about renting space at the vet's office.

The following list of your dog's major body parts starts at his head and works down to his rear:

- ✔ **Head:** The nose is set into something called the muzzle. Your Boxer's muzzle fits right into the skull, which is what holds the eyes and ears where they belong. At the top/back portion of the skull, you'll feel a fairly prominent ridge of bone. This bone corresponds to the little ridge of bone that is at the top/back of your own skull. In dogs, that bone is called the occiput.

- ✔ **Neck and shoulder:** Right behind the occiput is the crest of the neck. This is where the neck begins. The neck runs down into the shoulders. If you run your hand from the crest down the neck, your hand will come to a stop at the withers. Lots of people call that point the top of the shoulders, but you'll sound very hip if you say, "Oh, you mean here, right at my dog's withers?"

- ✔ **Back and sides:** Below the withers, is your Boxer's back. (Anatomy experts say that, technically, only a portion of what we call the dog's "back" is really that. But because we aren't anatomy experts, calling this whole area the "back" is just fine.) The back extends clear on to the dog's hips. The area on the dog's side, between where the rib cage ends and the pelvis begins, is called the *loin*. The part of the body above the hind legs, extending from the loin to the base of the tail at the buttocks, is called the *croup*. The buttocks are buttocks — no matter which species they're on — so they shouldn't be hard to locate on your dog.

- ✔ **Back legs:** Moving down from the buttocks, that upper area is the place that corresponds to your own thighs. The next area down is called the *lower thigh,* and below the lower thigh is the *hock joint.* Down from the hock is the *rear pastern.* Heading back up the rear leg on its bottom side, and between the upper and lower thigh, is the *stifle joint.* The stifle corresponds to our knee. That little claw-like thing near the bottom inside edge of the Boxer's leg is called a *dew claw.* (What the dew claw has to do with dew is beyond me, but it's actually an undeveloped toe that harks back far beyond the time when your Boxer's ancestors had even become wolves. And that, my friends, is far back!) Dew claws grow on the front legs as well, but don't panic if your dog doesn't have any dew claws. Most breeders remove them just a few days after the puppies are born.

✔ **Front legs:** Your Boxer's feet are fairly obvious and easy to find. Just above the Boxer's front feet is the area between the foot and the wrist, called the *pastern.* The *forearm* is the area between the wrist and the elbow. It hooks up to the upper arm, which connects to the bottom edge of the shoulder blade.

Check out Figure 8-1 for an illustration of a Boxer's anatomy.

When all the body parts hang together correctly so the dog moves like one collective unit, your dog is referred to as being *sound.* When you watch your Boxer move around with strength and ease and her legs move directly forward with purpose, you can then say, "My, my, isn't she a sound looking Boxer!"

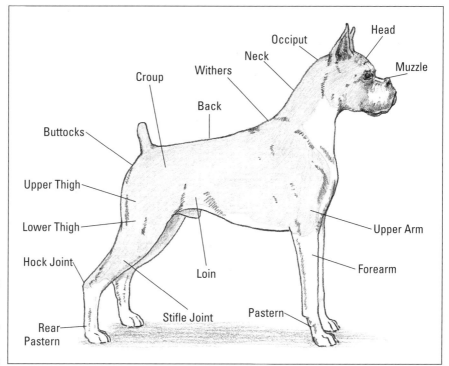

Figure 8-1:
The anatomy of a Boxer.

Getting Clear on Inherited Health Problems and Diseases

Like all breeds of domesticated dogs, including the mixed breeds, the Boxer has its share of hereditary problems. If you buy your Boxer from a reputable breeder, you're far less apt to see these problems in your dog, because a reputable breeder's stock is test-bred and rigidly selected to avoid these problems as much as possible. These complications do exist in the breed, however, and they should be discussed with the breeder from whom you purchase your dog. Even though your breeder constantly tests and does his best to breed around inheritable problems, breeders are not all-powerful, and occasionally one of these problems can arise in even the best planned litter.

If you ever suspect symptoms of these problems in your Boxer, make an appointment to see your veterinarian without delay.

Hip dysplasia

Hip dysplasia is an orthopedic problem that affects most large and many smaller breeds of dogs. A malformation of the hip joints, hip dysplasia usually occurs bilaterally, meaning in both hips. It can occur in varying degrees, from the mildest form (which is undetectable other than by x-ray) to extremely serious and painful cases, which require surgery.

Giving your Boxer a home checkup

To make sure your Boxer remains healthy, periodically perform your own little checkup on your dog. Neglecting to do so over extended periods of time can permit minor problems to develop into situations that require prolonged veterinary care and even expensive surgery. If you notice any abnormalities or anything that seems out of sorts, contact your vet:

- **Skin:** Your Boxer's skin should be free of eruptions or sores.

- **Coat:** Your Boxer's coat should be thick, lustrous, and clean.

- **Ears:** The ears should be clean, without an offensive odor.

- **Teeth:** Your Boxer's teeth should be white, without accumulated tartar.

- **Eyes:** The eyes should be clear and bright, with no discharge or irritation.

- **Nails:** Your Boxer's nails should be short, without cracks.

- **Anal glands:** The anal glands should be clear.

- **Anal temperature:** Check your Boxer's temperature whenever he appears out of sorts. A normal temperature is between 101.5 and 102 degrees.

Hair loss in dogs

Another condition possibly causing hair loss is *seasonal alopecia.* In simple terms, *alopecia* is hair loss. Seasonal alopecia, which usually appears on the flanks, occurs only during the winter. The hair grows back during the summer months. Have your vet examine your Boxer when this condition first occurs, because proper treatment can correct the problem.

Home remedies and hair-loss medications developed for humans should not be used on dogs, because they may not only be totally ineffective but, in some cases, they can prove toxic.

The normal hip can best be described as a ball and socket arrangement. The rear leg's upper bone (technically called the *femur*) has a head, which should fit neatly and firmly into the socket of the pelvis. A well-knit ball and socket allows the femur to rotate freely within the socket but is held firmly in place. When hip dysplasia exists, the socket is shallow, allowing the femur head to slip and slide to a greater or lesser degree. The more shallow the socket is, the more it impairs movement and causes pain.

Hip dysplasia (sometimes referred to by the acronym *HD*) is a condition that is considered to be *polygenetic,* which means it is created by the interaction of several genes, making it extremely hard to predict. Although it can be detected in the individual adult dog, it is only the law of averages that reduces the occurrence when breeding individual dogs who are clear of the problem.

Hypothyroidism

Hypothyroidism is a condition in which the thyroid gland malfunctions and its output is reduced. This condition occurs when an insufficient amount of thyroid hormone is produced by an underactive gland. Hypothyroidism appears in a good many of the larger breeds, including the Boxer.

The existence of hypothyroidism in an individual dog can be determined by a blood test. Poor hair growth is often one of the first signs of this disease. Overall lethargy and weakness are typical and, although appetite may decrease, weight gain continues. Thyroid hormone administered daily can control the disease, but medication may be necessary for the remainder of the dog's life.

The misconception about wild dogs

A common misconception about wild dogs is that they have no hereditary diseases or infirmities. But this is entirely untrue. There are documented cases of both canine and feline animals captured in the wild who have shown evidence of developing eye and bone abnormalities. Untreated, the afflicted animals would naturally perish. This only goes to prove that domesticated animals are not alone in developing genetic dysfunctions. The difference is that affected wild animals often don't survive long enough to breed.

Bloat

Bloat (technically called *gastric torsion*) occurs in many deep-chested dog breeds. The condition causes the stomach to rotate so that both ends are closed off. The food contained in the stomach ferments, but gases cannot escape, thereby causing the stomach to swell. This pressures the entire diaphragm and leads to extreme cardiac and respiratory complications. Affected dogs are in extreme pain and death can follow quickly unless the gas is released through surgery.

If you suspect your Boxer is suffering from bloat, contact your veterinarian immediately.

Cardiomyopathy

Cardiomyopathy is progressive deterioration of the heart muscle. It is frequently undetected, because dogs may not show any signs of the disease for years. As many as 80 percent of Boxers may be affected with cardiomyopathy or are carriers of the condition, which causes the affected dog to have an *arrhythmia* (irregular heartbeat). Although many dogs are without symptoms, some may have episodes of fainting or collapse, weakness, and occasionally heart failure. Death often occurs from an inability to control irregular heart rhythms and is usually sudden. The recommended method of diagnosis is through the use of the Holter monitor — a 24-hour electrocardiogram. The American Boxer Club is conducting an extensive study to help develop a DNA marker for this disease.

Sub-aortic stenosis

Sub-aortic stenosis (SAS) is a disease of the heart valve caused by a thickening of the tissue beneath the aortic valve. This thickening causes obstruction of

Checkups can stop check-writing

We humans have medical insurance because we know how staggering those hospital bills can be without it. Well, your Boxer's medical bills may not be quite as high as yours, but they won't be cheap. A good many of the causes for expensive treatment could be prevented by your own regular checkups. The old saw about "an ounce of prevention being worth a pound of cure" certainly applies here.

blood flow from the left side of the heart and may result in enlargement of the heart. Sub-aortic stenosis can ultimately cause heart failure. Mildly affected dogs may be free of symptoms and live normal lives. Severe cases can result in weakness, fainting, or sudden death. A murmur can usually be heard through a stethoscope. The diagnosis is made by echocardiogram (ultrasound).

Cancerous and benign tumors

Skin tumors are common in Boxers; however, a vast percentage of them are benign. Benign tumors appear at random on the body but do not spread by invading healthy organs. They do increase in size within themselves. In some cases where rapid growth is anticipated, benign tumors should be removed surgically.

Cancerous tumors can spread into adjacent areas of the body or they may release cells to form secondary tumors in other organs. Possible treatment for cancerous tumors includes removal through surgery, chemotherapy, and radiotherapy.

To Breed or Not to Breed?

Ah yes, that is the question. And my answer is . . . don't! Check out the following sections for information on breeding your Boxer and for reasons to spay or neuter your dog.

Looking at the reality of breeding

Before you even think further about the possibility of adding to the world's Boxer population, pay a visit to your local Humane Society or animal shelter. Across the country, thousands of purebred dogs are in need of rescue.

Unfortunately, a good percentage of these dogs are Boxers. The American Humane Society reports approximately 15 million healthy and friendly dogs and cats were euthanized in 1998 alone! Many of them were born into good homes but obviously fell into the hands of irresponsible owners.

You also have to give serious thought to the suitability of your Boxer for breeding. Not all Boxers, even those who are well bred, are suitable as breeding stock. If you discussed your plans to breed Boxers with the person from whom you purchased your dog, a responsible breeder will have undoubtedly selected a pup for you that was worthy of being bred. The operative word here of course is *worthy*. Your Boxer may be the smartest fellow to hit the boards since Lassie came home. He could be the most courageous and protective Boxer in town. And the dog may love you beyond all reason. But none of these are sound reasons for being a good candidate for producing offspring.

If the breeder from whom you purchased your Boxer sold the dog to you specifically as pet quality, the breeder obviously had no desire to have the dog bred. You should respect that experienced person's wishes. If you are unable to get in touch with the breeder, or if you doubt the credentials of the person from whom you purchased your dog, do some research and find a local breeder who has a reputation for producing show-quality Boxers. This person is the best one to advise you on whether your male or female should be bred.

All too often I hear people who have purchased purebred pets say, "Brandy needs to have a litter to complete her development," or "Jack needs a girlfriend to relieve his frustration." Believe me when I say that neither Brandy nor Jack need a sexual liaison to make their lives complete. Actually, especially in the case of Jack, or any other male, breeding will only serve to *increase* his frustration rather than relieve it.

Even if your Boxer is of the quality that warrants reproducing, you must consider the consequences of breeding. A litter of puppies can easily bring your dog population to eight or ten overnight. This situation can be great fun for your entire family for the first couple of weeks, when the puppies spend their lives nursing and sleeping. But the day will come very quickly when the mother of the puppies will look at you as if to say, "Well, you wanted puppies. Now take care of them!" It won't be long before the puppies will not only outgrow the whelping box, they'll outgrow the whole room they're in! Then, too, they will have transferred their dependence upon their mother to you, and they will want to be with you all the time! Think back on the patience and work involved in housebreaking and training your single Boxer puppy. Now multiply that by eight or ten.

We've talked about the need for properly socializing Boxer puppies. Not only will they object to being shunted off into the garage or the backyard, this will do nothing for their temperament. Boxer puppies must have continuous human contact from the moment they are born if they are to achieve their potential as companions. Ask yourself if you are willing to give them all the time they need and deserve until you have found a responsible home for each puppy in the litter. This may take weeks, sometimes months.

All too often, people are willing to commit to all the hard work and time involved in raising a litter of Boxers in anticipation of financial gain. They multiply the selling price of a hypothetical number of puppies by somewhere in the area of $600 to $800 and think, "Wow, what a great source of income!" Think again! Stop to consider the cost of a stud fee and prenatal veterinary expenses, then add the cost of possible whelping problems, health checks, tail docking, and ear cropping, and the necessary inoculation series and food for the puppies. These factors are all ones that put a very large dent in any anticipated profits. If you make a dollar, you'll be surprised! Good breeders do what they do for their love of the breed, not to become rich.

Being a responsible dog owner: Spaying or neutering your Boxer

Sexually altering your pet can also avoid some of the more distasteful aspects of dog ownership. Males who have not been neutered have the natural instinct to lift their legs and urinate on objects to mark the territory in which they live. Teaching an unneutered male not to lift his leg in your home can be extremely difficult. Plus, the unneutered male Boxer has that ongoing need to seek and find a girlfriend. He will have an even greater tendency to roam (if he stays home at all) if there is a female in heat in the area.

Females who have not been spayed have two estrus cycles each year, which are accompanied by a bloody discharge. Unless the female is kept confined, there will be extensive soiling of the area in which she is allowed, and, much more disastrous, she could become mismated and pregnant. Unspayed females also have a much higher risk of developing *pyometra,* or mammary cancer, later in life.

Spaying the female and neutering the male will not change the personality of your pet and will avoid many problems. Neutering the male Boxer can reduce his aggressive attitude toward other males and will reduce, if not entirely eliminate, his desire to pursue a neighborhood female who shows signs of an impending romantic attitude.

Spaying and neutering are not reversible procedures. If you are considering the possibility of showing your Boxer, keep in mind that altered animals are not allowed to compete in American Kennel Club conformation dog shows. Altered dogs may, however, compete in herding and obedience trials, agility events, and field trials.

Cropping Your Boxer's Ears, Removing His Dew Claws, and Docking His Tail

Normally, Boxer tails are docked and the dew claws are removed a day or two after birth, so that is something you won't have to concern yourself with. These procedures are attended to before the puppies' central nervous systems are fully developed, and they are accomplished with minimal pain and little or no bleeding. There are sound reasons for the removal of both, and I cover them in the following sections. You'll also find information here on cropping your Boxer's ears, so that you can decide whether to do this for your dog.

Removal of dew claws

Dew claws have no apparent function and are very easily ripped off in rough terrain, causing injury and great pain to the dog. At just a few days of age, dew claws are usually removed. The procedure is literally painless and takes just a few minutes to do. The pain it can save your dog down the road makes it very worthwhile.

Docking of tails

The breed standard of the Boxer calls for the tail to be docked and there is a good reason. Anyone who has lived with a Boxer knows what a happy extrovert the breed is. Every day is a celebration to a healthy Boxer, and holidays warrant celebrating to the maximum. A barometer of all that joy and enthusiasm is the Boxer's rear end and tail. They seemingly never stop their action.

Those of us who live with Boxers appreciate the thought that inspires the action behind undocked and incessantly whipping tails. But they can clear off low tables in a few wags and, even worse, tails can strike solid objects with such force that the dog's tail can be badly damaged or broken. Trying to heal a tail that never stops is a monumental task. The Boxer is far better off without his tail.

Cropping of ears

Typically, if a Boxer has a show career in his future, his ears are cropped. However, ear cropping is purely customary and cosmetic. The founders of the Boxer breed thought that ear cropping would give the dog a formidable look. But today there is no real need for this. Most people do think that cropping gives the Boxer the alert and elegant look that has long been a hallmark of the breed. But the choice is entirely yours. Many vets feel cropping results in fewer ear infections because it allows better oxygen supply to the external ear canal.

Whether to crop your Boxer's ears is a matter of choice best made by the individual owner, but the procedure should never be done by anyone other than a licensed veterinarian experienced in this area. Each veterinarian has her own feelings about when ear cropping should be done, but it usually falls between the ages of six and twelve weeks. At this age, the ear muscles have not yet developed and they are more easily trained to stand erect after cropping.

 All veterinarians who crop ears also have a regulated system of care and office visits that ensure success and avoid the possibility of infection. When it comes to ear cropping, be sure to follow your veterinarian's recommendations in all ways.

Choosing the Right Veterinarian for You and Your Boxer

No one knows more about the best veterinarian for your Boxer puppy than the breeder from whom you purchased the pup. If you are fortunate enough to live in the same area where your breeder lives, your problems are solved. You can continue right on with the vet who has known your puppy since birth.

 Having a veterinarian nearby is important, so that you can get to the vet in a hurry if you have to. As good as a veterinarian may be, if he or she lives hours away and you have an emergency situation, having to travel that distance may cost your dog's life.

Regardless of where you live, your breeder may be able to help by having friends or fellow dog breeders in your area provide recommendations. Your own neighbors may be able to help you in this respect as well. Check ahead before choosing a vet. Pay a visit to the recommended veterinarian before you bring your puppy home. Inspect the premises and discuss Boxer care with the vet. Some veterinarians have had little or no experience with Boxers and may even be intimidated by the prospect. If the facility and the person you speak to meet your approval, make an appointment to take your puppy there for her first checkup and insist that you see the same veterinarian each time your dog goes to the clinic. Some clinics have several veterinarians in attendance and it becomes the luck of the draw as to who will see your Boxer. If possible, you want to establish a history with one person, who will get to know your dog personally, not just read her file when you walk through the door.

 Veterinary visits can be traumatic enough for some dogs and being treated by a complete stranger each time can only add to a dog's anxiety. On the other hand, if your dog seems to dislike a particular vet, ask if you might be better off having someone else look at your dog instead.

Chapter 9

Feeding and Exercising Your Boxer

In This Chapter

▶ Figuring out what to feed your Boxer

▶ Changing your dog's diet as his nutritional needs change

▶ Making sure your Boxer gets enough exercise

*W*hen it comes to finding the best food for your Boxer, keep in mind that dogs are individuals, so what's right for one is not always right for another. Choosing the right dog food can be intimidating, so in this chapter, I guide you through the process. I also cover the importance of getting your Boxer the amount of exercise he needs to stay fit and trim. Food and exercise are two of the most important elements contributing to your dog's health. And this chapter gets you prepared to take care of your Boxer in the best way possible.

Knowing What Food to Feed and How Much Is Enough

Choosing a dog food and knowing how much to feed are two common questions for dog owners, especially those owning a dog for the first time. In the following sections, I let you know how to know what to feed your dog and I give you some suggestions for figuring out whether you're feeding enough (or too much).

Figuring out what to feed your Boxer

I have spoken with successful Boxer breeders in many parts of the world, and each person seems to have his own "tried-and-true, absolutely-the-best, under-no-circumstances-would-I-ever-change" method. Probably the best answer to this common question of what to feed your dog is: Feed what works best — not necessarily what the dog likes best but what keeps your dog looking and acting like a Boxer should.

Who can tell you just what food is best for your dog? The dog's breeder. Consult with the breeder from whom you purchased your Boxer in the first place whenever you have questions about your dog's nutrition. If the breeder's adult dogs were healthy and the puppies were healthy (and why would you buy from a breeder whose dogs weren't?), she knows what works when it comes to nutrition. So take her advice seriously.

All dogs are *carnivorous* (meat-eating) animals, and although the vegetable content of your dog's diet should not be overlooked, a dog's physiology and anatomy are based upon eating animal protein. Protein and fat are absolutely essential in a dog's diet.

The animal protein and fat your dog needs can be replaced by some vegetable proteins, but the amounts and the kind required in a vegetarian diet require a broad understanding of canine nutrition. The average dog owner seldom has that knowledge and even those who do are not inclined to spend the time needed to combine and/or cook the required ingredients. So what does this all mean? Whether canned or dry, look for a food in which the main ingredient is derived from meat, poultry, or fish. That way, you'll ensure your dog is getting the kind of protein he needs.

Many excellent commercial dog foods are available today. Manufacturers of the leading brands of dog food conduct extensive research to determine the exact ratio of vitamins and minerals necessary to maintain your dog's well-being. Research teams have determined the ideal balance of minerals, protein, carbohydrates, and trace elements for a dog's health. Dog food manufacturing has become so sophisticated that you can now buy food for dogs living almost any lifestyle, from sedentary to highly active. Be sure to read the packaging labels on dog foods carefully, or consult with your veterinarian, who will assist you in selecting the best moist or dry food for your Boxer.

You get what you pay for when it comes to dog food. Producing a nutritionally balanced, high-quality food that is easily digested by a dog costs more for the manufacturer than it costs to produce a brand that provides only marginal nourishment.

By law, all dog food labels must list all the ingredients in descending order by weight. (See Figure 9-1 for an example of a typical dog food label.) As in food for human consumption, the major ingredient is listed first, the next most prominent ingredient follows, and so on down the line. A diet based on meat or poultry (appearing first in the ingredients list) is going to provide more canine nutrition per pound of food than one that lists a filler grain product as the leading ingredient. The diet based on meat or poultry will also cost you more than a food that is primarily made of inexpensive fillers.

The use of vitamin supplements for dogs is highly controversial. Many breeders believe the high incidence of orthopedic problems modern dogs face are not entirely hereditary conditions but are exacerbated by overuse of vitamin supplements. Their suspicions are not without merit; most high-quality commercial dog foods are well balanced and highly fortified. Supplementation could easily throw that balance off and lead to growth problems. Before adding any supplement to the food you give your dog, discuss the product with both your breeder and your veterinarian. If you do decide to use a supplement, never exceed the prescribed dosage.

Knowing how much food to feed

The correct amount of food to maintain a Boxer's optimum condition varies as much from dog to dog as it does from human to human. I can't tell you how much to feed your dog any more than I can tell you how much *you* should eat every day. A great deal depends on how your dog is using up the calories she consumes. A Boxer who spends the entire day pounding the pavement doing police work needs considerably more food than the house dog whose exercise is limited to a leisurely walk around the block once a day.

Figure 9-1:
A dog food label lists the ingredients in descending order by weight.

Ingredients: Chicken, Corn Meal, Chicken By-Product Meal, Ground Grain Sorghum, Ground Whole Grain Barley, Chicken Meal, Chicken Fat (preserved with mixed Tocopherols, a source of Vitamin E, and Citric Acid), Dried Beet Pulp (sugar removed), Natural Chicken Flavor, Dried Egg Product, Brewers Dried Yeast, Potassium Chloride, Salt, Choline Chloride, Calcium Carbonate, DL-Methionine, Ferrous Sulfate, Vitamin E Supplement, Zinc Oxide, Ascorbic Acid (source of Vitamin C), Dicalcium Phosphate, Manganese Sulfate, Copper Sulfate, Manganese Oxide, Vitamin B_{12} Supplement, Vitamin A Acetate, Calcium Pantothenate, Biotin, Lecithin, Rosemary Extract, Thiamine Mononitrate (source of Vitamin B_1), Niacin, Riboflavin Supplement (source of Vitamin B_2), Pyridoxine Hydrochloride (source of Vitamin B_6), Inositol, Vitamin D_3 Supplement, Potassium Iodide, Folic Acid, Cobalt Carbonate.

Guaranteed Analysis:
Crude Protein not less than 26.0%
Crude Fat not less than 14.0%
Crude Fiber not more than................. 4.0%
Moisture not more than 10.0%

Animal feeding tests using Association of American Feed Control Official's procedures substantiate that this product provides complete and balanced nutrition for adult dogs.

A general guideline to keep in mind when it comes to how much to feed your dog is this: Feed your dog whatever amount she will eat readily within about 15 minutes of being given the meal. What your dog does not eat in those first 15 minutes should be taken up and discarded. Leaving food out for extended periods of time can lead to erratic and finicky eating habits.

Closely monitor your dog's condition to determine whether she's getting the correct amount of food. You should be able to feel (but not see) her ribs and backbone through a slight layer of muscle and fat. When in doubt, consult your veterinarian for suggestions.

Fresh water and a properly prepared balanced diet (containing all the essential nutrients in correct proportions) are all you need to feed your healthy dog. If your Boxer will not eat the food you offer her, she is either not hungry or does not feel well. If the former is the case, your dog will eat when she is hungry (dogs don't go on hunger strikes for very long). If you suspect your Boxer is not feeling well, make an appointment with your veterinarian.

A substance called *bile* is continually produced by the liver, but in some Boxers the bile is produced in an excessive amount at times. When this occurs, the dog usually loses interest in eating anything other than grass when she's allowed outdoors. Eventually vomiting occurs, and the system is set back in order.

Paying Attention to Your Boxer's Changing Nutritional Needs

Most top-level dog food manufacturers now produce special diets for weaning puppies, dogs who are growing, dogs whose weight needs to be maintained at the current level, dogs who are overweight, dogs who are underweight, and older dogs. Although the amount of these foods may remain the same as standard products, the calorie and nutritional content is adjusted to suit the particular level that accompanies each of these periods of a dog's life.

Using the correctly formulated food for each of these stages of your dog's life is very important. A food that is too rich can cause your dog just as many if not more problems than one that is not rich enough. Read the labels that appear on the can or box, study the promotional literature that is published by the manufacturer of the dog food you are considering, and seek the advice of those who are experienced with Boxers.

Puppy food

Protein is an important part of a puppy's diet. A good puppy diet consists of at least 20 percent protein. But protein is not the only thing necessary for your puppy's growth. Puppies also need fat, which has the calories that those little energy-burning bundles of joy need. Fat also results in healthy skin and helps build resistance to disease. Animal fats should make up approximately 10 percent of your puppy's diet. Carbohydrates also supply energy for your puppy. Potatoes, rice, and even pasta are good sources of carbohydrates. (If you prepare your own carbohydrates for your puppy, just be sure they are cooked well, because a young puppy won't be able to process them if they are not well done.)

Puppy foods must be easily digestible and contain all the important vitamins and minerals along with calcium and phosphorous, which are extremely important for bone growth. Calcium and phosphorus work together to do their job, but they must be present in the right proportions in order to be effective. Too little calcium can subject a young dog to bone deformities, such as *rickets*. And too much calcium is suspected of causing many of the bone diseases dog breeders are dealing with today.

Maintenance diets

As dogs mature, their exercise requirements decrease. If you just want to maintain the weight your dog is currently at, a maintenance diet is the one to try. Experiment with the amount you feed your dog, making sure his weight remains steady.

Food for older dogs

As your Boxer ages, getting out of bed in the morning is just as difficult for him as it is for aging humans. An older dog has less activity and a slower metabolism, but, like their aging owners, the elderly Boxer will probably still feel entitled to the same size of food portions. A food geared toward older dogs will enable you to feed your dog a substantial amount but still cut down on calories so that she doesn't gain weight (and end up with more serious health problems).

Meeting Your Boxer's Special Nutritional Needs

In some circumstances, your dog may need special food — for example, to help him get through health problems or lose weight. In the following sections, I take a look at diets that address both of these common problems.

Feeding the ailing Boxer

When your Boxer is under the weather, diet becomes a very important part of the recuperating process. Sick dogs need a diet that is low in carbohydrates but high in vitamins, minerals, and fat. Instead of attempting to mix food on your own to accomplish this end, you are much better off speaking to your vet about a prescription diet that is specially formulated for this purpose.

Some dogs have chronic gastrointestinal problems of various kinds that require an entirely different approach to nutrition. Normally speaking, dogs with conditions of this nature need food that is easily digestible but low in fat. Prescription diets are also recommended for dogs with gastrointestinal problems. As a general rule, speak to your veterinarian about foods if your Boxer is experiencing anything other than optimum health.

Feeding the overweight Boxer

Dogs, young or old, don't become obese overnight. The excess weight comes on gradually, and your eye may accustom itself to the gradual gains so that nothing seems out of the ordinary. If this is the case, periodic hops onto the scale can be very helpful for your dog. Your vet can advise you on how much your Boxer needs to lose and how you should go about helping your dog to lose that weight. Your Boxer may seem fit as a fiddle, but I still strongly suggest biannual visits to the vet's office for weight control and preventive maintenance. Most vets have scales made especially for weighing animals and will automatically have your Boxer hop on as part of their normal office procedure.

If your Boxer is not overeating and is getting sufficient exercise, and he has still gained weight, something else may be causing the weight gain. Your vet can — and should — look into this possibility.

Getting Your Boxer the Exercise She Needs

Exercise is something your Boxer needs and it is also something that will improve your *own* health and state of mind. Fortunately, you do not have to become a marathon runner to give your Boxer the exercise she needs. Walking at a pace that tells you you're doing something more than just slogging along is a good pace for both you and your dog.

If improving your health isn't incentive enough to get you out and moving, think about exercise this way: It's a nonprescription mood neutralizer for your dog. Although Boxers aren't classed among the high-strung breeds, their heritage is fraught with pursuits that required a better-than-average energy level. That energy doesn't just go away because you'd like it to. It will be used in *some* way, and if you would prefer that Roscoe does so by eating the sofa or taking down the wallpaper, that's your choice. But most Boxer owners would prefer to have their dog use up her energy by taking a good brisk walk, playing catch, or bringing back a Frisbee.

Both veterinarians and Boxer breeders caution against feeding a Boxer immediately before or after strenuous exercise, because they believe this can definitely lead to bloat, which is a life-threatening condition.

Don't expect your Boxer to get the exercise he needs on his own, unless another dog is around. And even then, the dogs probably won't be all that active after they emerge from puppyhood. As your Boxer matures, you'll find that he becomes less and less inclined to be self-starters in the exercise department. However, if *you* are involved, perhaps by throwing a toy to your dog (as shown in Figure 9-2), a Boxer of any age is ready, willing, and able to enjoy the activity right along with you. Always supervise your Boxer's exercise, and that way you'll be sure the dog is getting enough of the right kind.

Exercising your puppy

If you watch puppies at play with their littermates, you will note that they have frequent but brief bouts of high-level activity. These high-activity periods are nearly always followed by a good long nap. Puppies need exercise, but only as much as they themselves want to take. And they should be given ample time to rest after any period of activity.

Just as soon as you and your puppy master the collar and leash technique, the two of you can be off to explore the neighborhood and perhaps a nearby park (that is, of course, after all your pup's inoculations are up to date). A walk around the neighborhood gives you both the exercise you need, and when you're out and about, you'll be working on your tyke's socialization process as well.

Figure 9-2:
Playing
fetch is a
great way
for your
Boxer to get
exercise,
and it helps
to build
a great
relationship
between
you and
your dog.

Photograph courtesy of Richard Tomita

Don't expect a baby pup to take a ten-mile hike. The smart pup will plunk his little rear down and refuse to budge, and you'll have to tote the little fellow all the way back home. Your pup may want to please you by trying to keep up and exerting himself beyond what is reasonable, however. So always make sure you give your pup *brief* periods of exercise with lots of rest in between.

Getting your adolescent and healthy adult Boxer moving

When she's out of puppyhood, your Boxer will probably be able to out-walk you any day of the week and still be up for some fast-stepping aerobics accompanied by her favorite disco beat. She'll also be ready for every conceivable game you can think up and will probably want to continue on far longer than is good for either one of you. Just as you should do for yourself, whenever you start on a new form of exercise for your Boxer, do so gradually and increase the duration very slowly over time.

Don't jog with a young Boxer — at least not before the dog is at least 18 months of age. By then, the bones and muscles have formed and strengthened to the point where the jarring involved will not do permanent damage.

Many Boxers love to swim (see Figure 9-3), and there couldn't be any better exercise for you or your dog. Any place that is safe for *you* to swim will be safe for your Boxer as well, but never allow your Boxer to swim in a place that's too dirty or too dangerous for you. If you and your Boxer will be swimming in the ocean, make sure you understand the dangers involved and are aware of the areas in which riptides and undercurrents prevail. Boxers who love the water can be too adventurous for their own good. Make sure you don't send your pal into a dangerous situation.

Be extremely careful in hot weather, when it comes to exercising your Boxer. Confine exercise periods to the early morning hours (before temperatures rise) or the evening hours (after temperatures have dropped). Boxers absolutely cannot tolerate heavy exercise in high temperatures.

Regardless of your Boxer's age, be sensitive to bone or joint injuries sustained in exercise or playing games. Always inspect sore or tender areas, and if they seem particularly painful for the dog, see your vet right away. Concrete walkways and stony paths can be hard on a Boxer's feet. Inspect your dog's foot pads for cuts and abrasions often, especially if his exercise takes place on cement.

Figure 9-3:
Many Boxers love the chance to swim, as this one does in a backyard pool.

Helping your older Boxer exercise

Just because the old-timers have reached the twilight of their years doesn't mean they have to stop living! The older Boxer will still enjoy taking those walks with you every day. Maybe he won't be thrilled about heading outdoors on cold or blustery days, but when the weather is fair, there is absolutely no reason why the two of you can't be out there taking a nice leisurely walk around the block or down to the park. Don't push it, though. Keep in mind that your Boxer is older. Catching balls and Frisbees may be too much for an older dog, even if he thinks he's still capable of doing the 100-yard dash. Be kind and be careful with the old folks (human and canine), and they'll be with you for a long, long time.

Chapter 10

Preventing Health Problems in Your Boxer

In This Chapter

▶ Making sure your Boxer gets all his shots

▶ Grooming your Boxer — for health *and* beauty

▶ Maintaining a health log for your dog

*I*n this age of high medical costs, both human and animal, an ounce of prevention is most certainly worth a pound of cure. Pay attention to your Boxer and deal with problems as they arise — before they become serious.

Boxers are, by and large, a healthy breed. Compared to many other breeds, they are definitely low-maintenance. But this doesn't mean Boxer owners can be negligent. Boxers are living, breathing creatures who are subject to various accidents and ailments as they progress from puppyhood into adulthood. And it's your job to keep your Boxer free from as many of these problems as possible. In this chapter, I tell you how.

Getting Your Boxer the Inoculations She Needs

Vaccines work the same way in dogs as they do in humans — by introducing a minute amount of a disease into your dog's system so that the dog can build up an immune response to the disease. The dog is then able to ward off the disease if she is exposed to it at a later date. Diseases that were once fatal to almost all infected dogs are now very effectively dealt with through the use of vaccines. The danger of your Boxer being infected with distemper, hepatitis, hard pad, leptospirosis, or the extremely virulent parvovirus is unlikely, as long as the dog is properly inoculated and the recommended series of booster shots are given.

Cases of rabies among well-cared-for dogs is practically unheard of in the United States. Still, dogs who come in contact with wild animals of any kind can be at risk if they are not properly immunized. Even city dogs can encounter rats, squirrels, rabbits, bats, and many other small rodents, all of whom have been known to be carriers of rabies. So be sure to have your dog immunized.

All responsible breeders give their puppies at least one, if not two, temporary shots against infectious diseases before the puppies leave for their new homes. Your dog only has complete immunity after she has been given the complete series of inoculations at the prescribed intervals.

Every veterinarian has his own recommendation as to what age is appropriate for your dog to get her inoculations, so check with your vet on your dog's first visit and be sure to follow the vet's guidelines.

You aren't legally required to vaccinate your dog against any of the communicable diseases other than rabies. The rabies vaccine is not without risk in isolated cases, but the possibility of a negative reaction is far outweighed by the consequences of contracting the disease. Rabies can be transmitted to humans and is almost always fatal. It is *always* fatal to dogs.

Most boarding kennels and training groups will not accept your dog if you cannot furnish copies of your dog's immunization record or if the inoculations are not up to date. This requirement is enforced to protect the kennel owner and all of the dogs who are on the premises, including yours.

If you know your dog is sensitive to the multivaccine shots, insist on seeing the vial containing the vaccine your veterinarian uses before the inoculation is given. Many owners' hearts have been broken and pocketbooks emptied because veterinarians have cavalierly dismissed any concerns the owners have had.

Many puppies are extremely sensitive to the 5-, 6-, and 7-in-1 modified live vaccines (DHLPP). Some puppies get very ill within two or three days of receiving the vaccines, or even up to a couple of weeks later. In other cases, seizures or symptoms of hypothyroidism, liver and kidney problems, and heart complications show up several years later, to a greater or lesser degree. A good many breeders are recommending giving separate shots over a graduated period of time. Discuss this with the breeder from whom you purchased your Boxer puppy and insist your veterinarian follows those recommendations to the letter.

On rare occasions, some dogs do not, for one reason or another, develop full immunity against infectious diseases. So being able to detect signs of these illnesses is important, in case your Boxer is one of the rare dogs who does not become completely immune and actually does develop one of these diseases. In the following sections, I give you the information you need on each of the major diseases against which your dog should be inoculated.

Canine parvovirus

Parvovirus (commonly referred to as *parvo*) is a particularly infectious gastrointestinal disease. Dogs can contract the disease through direct contact with dogs who have it or by being exposed to areas in which infected dogs have been housed. Although dogs of all ages can be and are infected by canine parvovirus, this disease is particularly fatal to puppies.

Symptoms include acute diarrhea, often bloody, with yellow- or gray-colored stools. Soaring body temperatures, sometimes as high as 106 degrees, are not uncommon in dogs suffering from parvovirus, particularly puppies. Death can follow as quickly as one to three days after the first symptoms appear, making early treatment critical. If you suspect your dog may have this disease, contact your veterinarian *immediately.*

Canine virus distemper

An extremely high fever can be the first sign of distemper, a very serious and often fatal disease. Mortality rates among puppies and adults who have not been immunized is extremely high. Other symptoms may be loss of appetite, diarrhea, blood in the stools, and eventually dehydration. Respiratory infections of all kinds are apt to accompany these conditions. Symptoms may appear as quickly as a week after exposure.

Hardpad

Considered to be a secondary infection, hardpad often accompanies distemper. The main symptom is a hardening of the pads of a dog's feet, but the virus eventually attacks the central nervous system, causing convulsions and encephalitis.

Infectious hepatitis

Infectious canine hepatitis is a liver infection of particularly extreme strength. It is a different virus than the hepatitis that affects humans, but the canine version multiplies in the lymphatic system and then damages the blood vessels and liver cells. A very high percentage of recovered dogs have also been found to have kidney damage. Infectious hepatitis eventually affects many other parts of a dog's body with varying degrees of intensity so that the infected dog can run the entire range of reactions, from watery eyes, listlessness, and loss of appetite to violent trembling, labored breathing, vomiting, and extreme thirst. Infection normally occurs through exposure to the urine of animals infected with the disease. Symptoms can appear within a week of exposure.

The great vaccination debate

In all parts of the world, debates rage over whether a dog should continue to receive inoculations against infectious diseases on an annual basis after the important first year. (These continuing inoculations are sometimes referred to as *booster shots.*) Strong evidence is available to substantiate both contentions. Those opposed to yearly vaccinations cite occurrences of chronic health problems, sterility, and aborted litters as a result of overadministration of the vaccines. VaxTrax, a titer sponsored by Cornell University, is used to see if a dog needs a booster for the distemper, corona, and Parvo virus, instead of just giving the dog a yearly booster whether he needs it or not. Those who oppose abolishing the booster shots argue that cases in which dogs suffer negative consequences to being vaccinated represent such a small percentage of the vaccinated population,

and the benefits of vaccination are so great, that not vaccinating is risky.

Some risk *does* exist in administering any vaccine. How that risk stands against the possible loss of a dog through omitting the inoculations is a question that can be answered only by the individual dog owner.

As you weigh this issue with your vet, keep in mind that many of the infectious diseases (the distemper virus leading them all) ran rampant before the vaccines were developed. In many cases, contracting the diseases meant certain death. Vaccines do, according to new research, have a longer term of effectiveness than previously believed, however. So some vets are going to a two- or three-year interval between the time when the first shots are given and the time when revaccination is appropriate.

Leptospirosis

Leptospirosis (often called *lepto*) is a bacterial disease contracted by direct exposure to the urine of an animal infected with the disease. Both wild and domestic animals are affected by leptospirosis. And an animal can contract the disease simply by sniffing a tree or bush on which an infected animal has urinated. So vaccination is especially important.

Leptospirosis is not prevalent in all sections of the country, so the problem should be taken up with your veterinarian, particularly if you intend to travel with your dog. Lepto can be contagious to humans as well as animals and can be fatal to both. Rapidly fluctuating temperatures, total loss of maneuverability, bleeding gums, and bloody diarrhea are all symptoms. The mortality rate for those suffering from this disease is extremely high.

Rabies

Rabies infection normally occurs through a bite from an infected animal. All mammals are subject to infection. The rabies virus affects the dog through inflammation of the spinal cord and central nervous system. Rabies symptoms may not be as quick to appear or as detectable as the symptoms of other diseases, because the symptoms of rabies often resemble the symptoms of other less virulent diseases. Withdrawal, personality change, excessive salivating, and progressive paralysis are common symptoms as well as the myriad of symptoms accompanying the other infectious diseases, including convulsions and complete loss of manueverability.

Most breeders recommend that the puppy owner wait as long as possible to give a rabies shot — up to one year of age if at all possible.

Humans bitten by any animal suspected of being rabid should seek the advice of their personal physician at once. If your dog is bitten by an animal that you suspect may have rabies, call your veterinarian without delay.

Keeping your dog's rabies inoculations current and attaching to your dog's collar the tag issued by your veterinarian are both extremely important. If your dog ever bites someone, you must be able to offer proof of current rabies inoculation. If not, your dog may, by law, be held in quarantine for a considerable length of time to determine the possibility of rabies infection.

Bordatella (kennel cough)

Although Bordatella (commonly referred to as *kennel cough*) is highly infectious, it is actually not a serious disease. Kennel cough can be compared to a mild case of the flu in human beings. Infected dogs act and eat normally. The main symptom of the disease, a persistent hacking cough, is far worse than the disease itself. The name of the disease is misleading, because it leads people to believe that a dog must be exposed to a kennel environment in order to be infected. Actually, the disease can easily be passed on from one dog to another through even casual contact.

In severe cases of kennel cough, antibiotics are sometimes prescribed in order to avoid secondary infections such as pneumonia. But various protective procedures have been developed that can be administered by your veterinarian. An intranasal vaccine is available, which provides immunity.

If your dog visits a dog park or is taken to a boarding kennel where he comes into contact with other dogs, be sure he has had the bordatella vaccine. Most boarding kennels now insist upon proof of protection against kennel cough before they will accept a dog for boarding.

Watching Out for Parasites

Parasites can invade your Boxer both internally and externally. And at least one form of parasite attacks both internally and externally. Cleanliness, regular grooming, and biannual stool examinations by your veterinarian can keep the infestations down, but don't be upset or surprised to find that, even with the best of efforts on your part, some of these nasty creatures will find their way into your home or inside your Boxer's skin or stomach.

The following sections guide you through the different parasites your Boxer may encounter and let you know how to treat them if they become a problem for your dog.

External parasites

External parasites are the ones most people have heard of — fleas, lice, ticks, and mange. But even though they're common, treating them is still very important.

Fleas

No matter how careful and fastidious you may be in the care of your Boxer, fleas can still become a problem. Your dog can bring fleas into your home just by playing in the yard or going on daily walks. And once they're there, the little creatures multiply with amazing speed. Cats with outdoor access compound this already difficult problem by attracting fleas on their neighborhood patrols and bringing them back home on their fur.

Those who live in northern climates get a winter respite from the flea problems because of the heavy frosts and freezing temperatures, which fleas cannot survive. People who live in warmer climates face the flea problem year-round.

Unfortunately, flea baths do not solve the flea problem. If you find even one flea on your dog, undoubtedly hundreds, and maybe even thousands, are lurking in the carpeting and furniture throughout your home. The minute you finish giving your Boxer his bath, the fleas are ready and able to return to him as he walks through the home.

Aside from the discomfort flea bites cause your dog, the severe scratching they induce can cause *hot spots*. Hot spots are created when a dog chews and scratches so hard that the skin is broken. If hot spots are not attended to promptly, they can form moist, painful abscesses and all the hair surrounding the area falls off.

When your home and dog have been infested with fleas, there is only one surefire way of eliminating the problem and keeping it in check. This approach takes a bit of prior planning but it's well worth the time:

1. **Make an appointment for your Boxer to be given a flea bath by your veterinarian or groomer.**

   Most groomers use products that will completely rid your Boxer of existing fleas.

2. **While the dog is away being bathed, have a commercial pest control service come to your home.**

   If you bring your dog home before you have your home treated, the fleas will be back on your dog within hours. The service will spray both the interior of your home and the surrounding property as well. Most pest control companies guarantee the effectiveness of their work for several months.

3. **The day after your Boxer comes home from his bath, apply an insect growth regulator to the dog.**

   These new flea control products can be used on a monthly basis or year-round. They control fleas by stopping their life cycle. The benefit of these products is that they have no deadly effect on mammals at all. You can give your dog pills or you can use the liquids, which you place on the dog's skin between the shoulder blades. Administered regularly, these preventives are proving to be highly effective in keeping both fleas and ticks off of household pets.

Although the home spraying measure does provide a solution to flea problems, the operation does have a down side. You must vacate your home and keep it closed for at least a few hours following the spraying. Also, the toxicity buildup of the chemicals used should be considered. Some services are now using a nontoxic method, which is a great alternative.

Fleas also act as carriers of the tapeworm eggs. When a dog swallows a flea, the tapeworm eggs grow in the dog's intestines. Unfortunately, if your dog has fleas, he will almost invariably have tapeworms. Check out "Internal parasites" for a discussion of tapeworms.

Lice

Well-cared-for Boxers seldom encounter a problem with lice, because these parasites are spread through direct contact. A dog must spend time with another animal who has lice or be groomed with a contaminated brush or comb in order to be at risk.

If no fleas are present and you suspect lice, bathe your dog with an insecticidal shampoo every week until the problem is taken care of. Lice live and breed exclusively on the dog itself, so it is not necessary to treat the area in which the dog lives.

Ticks

If you live near a wooded area, you are bound to run across at least the occasional tick. In fact, your Boxer can pick up these parasites just running through grass or brush. Ticks are bloodsucking parasites that bury their heads firmly into a dog's skin. The ticks gorge themselves on the dog's blood and then find a dark little corner in which to lay their eggs — thousands of them at a time.

 Some of the same insect growth regulators that control fleas also do an excellent job of keeping ticks off your dog. I can attest to their effectiveness. I live at the edge of a huge forested track, and my dog and I take hikes through the woods constantly. He comes home tick-free and, more often than not, I'm picking the little varmints off *my* body.

 Ticks represent a serious health hazard to both humans and other animals. Ticks in some areas carry Lyme disease and Rocky Mountain spotted fever. The entire area in which the dog lives must be aggressively treated against ticks with sprays and dips made especially for the purpose of removing ticks.

To remove a tick from your dog's body, first soak the tick with a tick removal solution that can be purchased at most pet stores. When the tick releases its grip, you can remove it with a pair of tweezers. Be sure that the tick loosens its grip before you attempt to remove it. Otherwise, you may allow the head to break away from the tick. If the tick's head is allowed to remain lodged in the dog's skin, it could cause a severe infection. After the tick is removed, swab the area with alcohol to avoid infection.

 Do not flush the tick in the toilet, because it may survive the swim! Do not crush the little beast between your fingers because that will expose you to whatever disease the tick may be carrying. The best way to eliminate a tick permanently is to put it in a jar with a bit of alcohol and then screw the lid on tightly.

 Always wear latex gloves and use tweezers to avoid the possibility of infecting yourself, in case the tick is a disease carrier. Wash your hands and any instruments you've used with alcohol as well. If you suspect your area to be infested with disease-carrying ticks, put the tick in a bottle or plastic bag and take it to your vet without delay for testing.

Mange

Although the word *mange* may strike a note of terror in the hearts of most people, it is a treatable condition. There are two kinds of mange — *demodectic* and *sarcoptic*. Both types are caused by mites and must be treated by your veterinarian.

Demodectic mange is believed to be present on practically all dogs without creating any undue harm to the affected dog. Only about one percent of all dogs ever develop clinical symptoms of this form of mange. Demodectic mange comes in two varieties: local and general. Dogs affected locally may lose the hair around their eyes and in small patches on their chest and forelegs. Local demodectic mange can easily be treated by a veterinarian and must not be neglected, because on rare occasions the local form can develop into the more severe, generalized form.

Sarcoptic mange is also known as *scabies* and can be present over the entire dog. Symptoms include loss of hair on the legs and ears, as well as hair loss in patches over the entire body. Your veterinarian must do a skin scraping to identify the type and prescribe the appropriate treatment. Weekly bathing with medications especially formulated for this parasite can usually eliminate the problem. This type of mange is passed on by direct contact and is highly contagious. It can cause a skin irritation in humans who have had close contact with the infected animal.

Cheyletiellosis

Cheyletiellosis is a parasitic disease of the dog's skin that is commonly referred to as *walking dandruff.* In many cases the condition is first noted by humans because it causes intense but temporary irritation and itching to those who come in direct contact with the affected dog. Cheyletiellosis is easily and effectively treated with prescription shampoos or by Ivermectin inoculations.

Internal parasites

The most common internal parasites are roundworms, tapeworms, and heartworms. All three are best diagnosed and treated by your veterinarian. Great advances are continually being made in dealing with these parasites. What used to be complicated, messy, and time-consuming treatments have been replaced and simplified over the years.

Tapeworms

Tapeworms are a part of the life cycle of the flea. If your Boxer has fleas or has had them in the recent past, you will undoubtedly have to deal with tapeworms. Small rice-like segments of the worm are often found crawling around the dog's anus or in the stool just after the dog has relieved herself. Periodic stool examinations done by your veterinarian can determine the presence of tapeworms, even though you may not observe the segments yourself. Your vet can administer an injection that quickly and completely eliminates the problem.

Heartworms

Heartworms are parasitic worms found in dogs' hearts. The worm is transmitted by mosquitoes that carry the larvae of the worm. Dogs are the only mammals that are commonly affected, and the condition is far more prevalent in warmer climates, which have longer periods of time in which mosquitoes can reproduce. Blood tests can detect the presence of this worm and a veterinarian can prescribe both preventive and corrective measures for this parasite, which can be administered to the dog orally.

Regular stool examinations by your veterinarian will keep your Boxer free of most worms. Testing for heartworms, however, requires a blood test.

If you and your Boxer live in an area where heartworm can be a problem, ask your vet if your dog should be put on heartworm preventive. However, *do not* give your Boxer heartworm medicine until your vet has completed the necessary testing. The preventive medication for dogs free of heartworm is different from that administered to dogs who have already been infected. Giving the infected dog the preventive medication can cause serious illness and even death.

Whipworms and hookworms

Whipworms and hookworms are shed in a dog's stool and can live for long periods in the soil. Both can attach themselves to the skin of humans as well as animals and eventually burrow their way to the lining of the intestines. They are then seldom passed or seen. These two worms are only detected by microscopic examination of the stool and each worm requires specific medication to ensure elimination.

Roundworms

Not an unusual condition, roundworms are seldom harmful to adult dogs. However, these parasites can be hazardous to the health of puppies if they are allowed to progress unchecked. Roundworms are transmitted from a mother to her puppies, so responsible breeders make sure their females are free of worms before they are ever bred. Roundworms can sometimes be visible in a dog's stool but are easily detected in a microscopic examination of a fresh stool sample by your veterinarian. The coats of puppies affected by roundworms are usually dull looking and the puppy himself is thin in appearance but has a potbelly.

Grooming Your Boxer for Health and Beauty

Grooming is a great way for you and your Boxer to get comfortable with each other. Plus, it's a good chance for you to examine your dog's coat and body for any abnormalities or problems so that you can alert your vet if necessary.

Boxers shed their coats just like longhaired breeds do. The fallen hair is just far less noticeable with Boxers. If you're in doubt, just allow your Boxer to sleep on a white or light-colored sofa or chair on a regular basis, and you'll be amazed at the amount of hair that leaves the Boxer's body in just a few days' time.

Brushing

Frequent brushing removes old dead hair, cleans and massages the skin, and allows new hair to come in easily. The rubber curry comb is the ideal grooming aid for this project and this regular "massage" will be something your Boxer will soon look forward to. Brushing should always be done in the same direction as the hair grows. Begin at the dog's head and move toward the tail, then down the sides and legs. This procedure will loosen the dead hair and brush it off the dog. A chamois cloth, which can be purchased at most hardware stores, can be used to finish off your brushing job. This final touch will produce a high luster on your dog's coat.

If you brush your dog regularly, you won't need to bathe him very often, unless he has been off on a treasure hunt and found his way into something that leaves his coat with a disagreeable odor. Even then, many products are available (in both dry and liquid forms) that eliminate odors and leave the coat shiny and clean. You can find them at any pet store. A damp washcloth can also clean off even a Boxer who has given herself a mud bath.

 If your Boxer's coat becomes wet in cold weather, be sure to towel-dry the dog thoroughly. Check the skin inside the thighs and armpits to see if those areas are dry or red. Artificial heat during winter months can dry out the skin and cause it to become chapped. Place a small amount of Vaseline or baby oil on the palms of your hands and rub your hands over the dry areas as needed.

A grooming table, which puts your dog at a comfortable working level, saves your back and keeps your dog still while you attend to him. These tables can be purchased from any pet supply dealer or can be built at home. Trying to groom your dog while he is standing on the ground is difficult at best, because the dog will be inclined to pull away from what he doesn't like. And you'll have to hang on with one hand while you work with the other.

Ears

The Boxer's ears are very sensitive and a sore ear can make an otherwise happy fellow cross and cranky. Keeping ears clean is a simple job, but be sure never to prod into the ear any farther than you can see.

Dampen a cotton swab with warm water, squeeze out any excess liquid, and clean out all areas inside the ear that you can see. Be careful not to injure any of the delicate ear tissues by prodding or poking. If you ever smell a foul odor emanating from the ear, schedule an appointment with your vet without delay.

Teeth

If you give your Boxer those big, hard dog biscuits or large knuckle bones to chew on, chances are her teeth are in great shape. Chewing helps keep tartar and plaque from forming. Buildup of either of these substances can cause extensive and permanent damage to your dog's teeth and gums.

Brushing your dog's teeth on a regular basis can prevent tooth decay or dental tartar, which can lead to gingivitis. You can also keep your dog from having to undergo anesthesia and have her teeth cleaned by your veterinarian. Not only is this costly for you, but any time your dog is anesthetized, you run some risk.

So how do you brush a Boxer's teeth? Just like you would your own or like you would a small child's. It's really quite simple. For an illustration of the correct way to brush a dog's teeth, see Figure 10-1.

Start brushing your dog's teeth when she's a puppy, and she'll be used to it right away. Your local pet store has supplies like special toothpastes and toothbrushes that are geared for dogs.

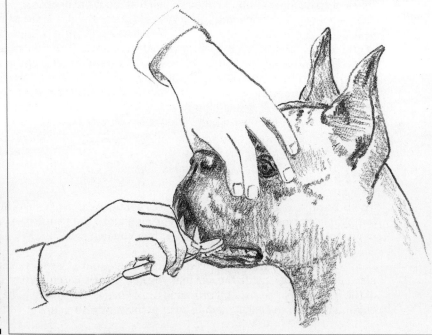

Figure 10-1:
Brushing your Boxer's teeth on a regular basis will keep her teeth and gums healthy for a lifetime.

Never use your own toothpaste on your dog. Dogs can't rinse and spit the way we do, and eating the human toothpaste could cause problems for your Boxer. Special dog toothpastes are available, but canine dentists say that the most important part is the actual brushing action, not which paste you use.

Eyes

If your Boxer's eyes appear red and inflamed, check for foreign bodies such as dirt or weed seeds. Flushing the dog's eyes with cotton and cool water or a sterile saline solution will usually eliminate foreign matter.

If irritation persists and your dog's eyes remain red, or if an unusually colored mucous is present, these could be symptoms of *conjunctivitis* (an eye disease that is highly contagious). Consult your veterinarian if you think your dog may have conjunctivitis.

Feet and nails

Always inspect your Boxer's feet for cracked pads. Check between the toes for splinters and thorns. Pay particular attention to any swollen or tender areas.

In many sections of the country, a weed called *foxtail* grows. This weed has a barbed hook-like portion that carries its seed. This hook easily finds its way into a Boxer's foot or between his toes and very quickly works its way deep into the dog's flesh, quickly causing soreness and infection. Foxtails should be removed by your veterinarian before serious problems result.

To keep your Boxer's feet compact and well arched, you need to keep his nails trimmed regularly. Long nails can cause your Boxer's feet to become flat and spread, which is not only unattractive but also unhealthy for your dog, because the long nails can become deformed and cause a great deal of pain. Check out Figure 10-2 for illustrated instructions for trimming your Boxer's nails.

Do not allow the nails to become overgrown and then expect to easily cut them back. Each nail has a blood vessel running through the center called the *quick*. The quick grows close to the end of the nail and contains very sensitive nerve endings. If the nail is allowed to grow too long, you won't be able to cut the nail back to a proper length without cutting into the quick. And cutting into the quick causes severe pain to the dog and can also result in a great deal of bleeding, which can be very difficult to stop. Always proceed with caution and remove only a small portion of the nail at a time.

Figure 10-2: Trimming your Boxer's nails regularly keeps his feet healthy and free of pain.

If your Boxer is getting plenty of exercise on cement or rough, hard pavement, the nails may keep sufficiently worn down. But if the dog spends most of his time indoors or on grass when he's outside, the nails can grow long very quickly.

Trim your dog's nails with canine nail clippers, an electric nail grinder (also called a *drumel*), or a coarse file made expressly for that purpose. All three of these items can be purchased at major pet stores. I prefer the electric nail grinder above the other methods of trimming nails, because the tool is so easy to control and completely avoids cutting into the quick. The Boxer's black nails make seeing where the quick ends impossible.

If you use the electric grinder, you need to introduce your puppy to it at an early age. The instrument has a whining sound not unlike a dentist's drill. The noise combined with the vibration of the sanding head on the nail itself can take some getting used to, but most dogs I have used it on eventually accept it as one of life's trials. My dogs have never liked having their nails trimmed, no matter which device I use. So my eventual decision was to use the grinder, because I was less apt to damage the quick.

If you do nip the quick in the trimming process, you can use any number of blood-clotting products that are available at pet stores. These products almost immediately stop the flow of blood where you've cut into the quick. Keep one of these products on hand in case you have a nail trimming accident or the dog breaks a nail on his own.

Anal glands

The anal glands are located on each side of a dog's anus. Their secretion serves as a scent that identifies each individual dog. These glands can become blocked, causing extreme irritation and even abscesses in the more advanced cases.

If you notice your Boxer pulling herself along the ground in a sitting position, check her anal glands. Contrary to popular belief, this habit is more apt to be the result of anal gland problems than of worms. Although not a particularly pleasant part of grooming your dog, if they're regularly attended to, the glands will stay clear and relatively easy to deal with. Performing this function as part of the bath can be less awkward.

To clean your dog's anal glands, place the thumb and forefinger of one hand on either side of the anal passage. Hold an absorbent cloth or large wad of cotton over the anus with your other hand. Exert pressure to both sides of the anus with your thumb and forefinger, allowing the fluid to eject into the cloth you are holding. The glands will empty quickly. If you're unsure how to perform this procedure or if your Boxer seems unusually sensitive in this area, seek the assistance of your veterinarian or groomer.

Setting Up a Health and Grooming Log

Keep a record book alongside your grooming table to note any problems you observe with your dog. If you note anything different in your Boxer's behavior or appearance, jot it down. If the situation develops into one that needs your vet's attention, record what the vet did and when. If veterinary care is necessary at a later date, you may be able to assist your vet in making a diagnosis with the notes you have made in your dog's medical book.

Your Boxer should have an annual checkup at the vet's office. Take your book along to scan while you're waiting. You may be reminded of problems or concerns that you can bring up with the vet. And this could prove invaluable in avoiding any future problems. This kind of record book is a good place to keep your dog's veterinary health and shot records as well. That way, you'll be aware of which inoculations are due and the dates they should be given. Most veterinarians keep computer records of their patients and automatically notify owners of necessary follow-up treatment, but staying on top of this important part of owning a dog is a good idea. Keep your own record of when your dog needs heartworm and stool checks or when booster inoculations are required.

Chapter 11

Being Prepared for Emergencies

*N*o matter how careful you are about keeping your Boxer safe, dogs, like children, have the ability to get themselves into scrapes that you could never anticipate. Accidents happen. We can be as careful as the day is long, but we can't protect our dogs from the world at large. Although veterinarians are there to help us in these times of emergency, you may encounter an occasion when immediate care is critical. I hope you never have to resort to home emergency care, but if it's necessary and you aren't prepared, it could mean your dog's life. In this chapter, you get all the information you need. Read it before an emergency strikes, and reread it periodically to refresh your memory. Because in a true emergency, you probably won't have time to read instructions.

Putting Together a First Aid Kit

The following list includes the basics for a well-stocked first aid kit. Remember to check the kit regularly to make sure that any liquids have not evaporated and that materials that may have been used are replaced.

✔ Activated charcoal tablets

✔ Adhesive tape (1- and 2-inch width)

✔ Antibacterial ointment (for skin and eyes)

✔ Antihistamine (approved by your vet for allergic reactions)

- ✔ Bandages and dressing pads (gauze rolls, 1- and 2-inch width)
- ✔ Blanket (for moving injured dog or warming)
- ✔ Cotton balls
- ✔ Diarrhea medicine
- ✔ Dosing syringe
- ✔ Eyewash
- ✔ Emergency phone numbers (taped on the cover of the first aid kit)
- ✔ Hydrogen peroxide (3 percent solution)
- ✔ Ipecac syrup (to induce vomiting)
- ✔ Nylon stocking (to use as muzzle)
- ✔ Petroleum jelly
- ✔ Pliers or tweezers (for removal of stings, barbs, and quills)
- ✔ Rectal thermometer
- ✔ Rubber gloves
- ✔ Rubbing alcohol
- ✔ Scissors (preferably with rounded tips)
- ✔ Tourniquet kit
- ✔ Syringe (without needle for administering oral medications)
- ✔ Towel
- ✔ Tweezers
- ✔ White sock (to slip over injured paw)

Ask your vet for special recommendations about which items should be a part of your home first aid kit. She may have a special device or product you may not have thought of.

If you have children, you probably keep a list of emergency phone numbers posted next to your telephone. But if your Boxer is your only child and you haven't already done so, sit down and write out this important list today. Include on it your regular veterinarian's phone number along with that of the nearest 24-hour emergency veterinary hospital. The number of your local poison control center should also be a part of this list as well.

Also include the number for the National Animal Poison Control Center (a division of the American Society for the Prevention of Cruelty to Animals). This agency provides expert 24-hour guidance on how to treat your Boxer until you can contact your own veterinarian. Call 888-426-4435 if you want the $45 charge (per case) billed to your credit card. Call 900-680-0000 to have it billed directly to your telephone bill.

Calling the Vet When Necessary

If you are in doubt about how best to handle any health problem, do not hesitate to pick up the phone and consult your veterinarian. In most cases, your vet knows which questions to ask and will be able to determine whether he needs to see your dog.

If any of the following symptoms occur, call your vet immediately:

- Blood in the stool
- Limping, trembling, or shaking
- Abscesses, lumps, or swellings
- Dark or cloudy urine
- Difficult urination
- Loss of bowel or bladder control
- Deep red or white gums
- Persistent coughing or sneezing
- Loss or impairment of motor control
- Gasping for breath
- Chronic vomiting
- Chronic diarrhea
- Continued listlessness
- Loss of appetite
- Excessive thirst
- Runny nose
- Discharge from eyes or ears

Your veterinarian will be able to tell you what to watch for and whether you should bring the dog in. Sometimes these symptoms represent nothing more than minor ailments, but they can also mean your dog is at risk for something more serious.

All dogs ingest something at one time or another that can cause vomiting or diarrhea. Vomiting or diarrhea do not necessarily mean that your dog is seriously ill, but if either symptom persists, never hesitate to call your veterinarian. Dogs often purge their digestive tracts by eating grass, which induces vomiting. Puppies often vomit when they have eaten too much or too fast. Mother dogs who are attempting to wean their puppies often eat and then regurgitate their food for the puppies. Nervousness or fright can induce vomiting, or in some dogs these reactions can cause diarrhea. None of this behavior is cause for alarm unless it occurs repeatedly.

Occasional diarrhea is best treated by switching your dog's regular diet to thoroughly cooked rice with a very small amount of boiled chicken. Keep your dog on this diet until the condition improves and then gradually add your dog's regular food over a period of several days.

Responding in Emergency Situations

You aren't a veterinarian, and the information in this section is not meant to be a substitute for the knowledge and experience your own vet has spent a lifetime accumulating. Having said that, keep in mind that any knowledge you can gather may prevent relatively minor situations from developing into serious complications. In some situations, intervention on your part may keep your dog alive until you can get to a veterinary hospital.

Every dog owner should know basic lifesaving techniques, and I cover them in this section. Always exercise extreme care in dealing with very ill or injured animals, however. Don't forget that where you and I use our hands as an automatic response to pain, a dog will use his mouth. Muzzling a dog in an emergency situation is often one of the best things you can do for everyone involved, including the dog.

Muzzling

Your Boxer loves you beyond all reason and would never think of biting you intentionally, but any animal can snap in reaction to pain. Muzzling your dog when administering treatment other than brushing or normal day-to-day grooming procedures is always a good idea. Getting your Boxer used to being muzzled will only help your dog feel more calm if you need to muzzle him in an emergency situation.

I use a discarded women's nylon stocking as a muzzle, because it's strong and won't cut or irritate the dog. Snugly rap the center section of the stocking twice around the dog's muzzle. Do not wrap so tightly that you cause the dog to be uncomfortable, but wrap firmly enough to keep your dog from using his jaws to bite. Tie the two remaining ends under the jaw and draw them back behind the dog's ears, tying them there.

Moving an injured dog

Moving an injured dog the size of a grown Boxer can be a challenge, especially if you are alone. Ideally, you'll have someone on hand to assist you. Lay the injured dog on a large towel or blanket, which you and the person assisting you can lift by the edges and transport to an open automobile.

Canine health insurance

Canine health insurance is offered to help owners withstand the cost of the new and costly advances in veterinary procedures. The policies range from excellent to practically useless. As the Romans used to say when they were hustling medical insurance, "Caveat emptor." Let the buyer beware. Read any insurance policy carefully, and find out whether the veterinarian you will be using honors such coverage.

If you are alone and cannot lift your dog by yourself, move the dog onto the blanket and slide the blanket along the ground until the dog is out of harm's way or until you reach your waiting vehicle. Hopefully, you'll be able to attract someone's attention to assist you in lifting the dog into your car. If not, do your best to move the dog into the car with as little disturbance as possible.

Burns

Minor burns can be treated by applying cold water or a cold compress. Gauze pads can be used to apply an antibiotic cream. Cover the burn with a gauze pad that can be held in place with an elastic bandage. Serious burns or scalding need your veterinarian's attention at once. Cool burned areas with very cool water or cover with water-soaked towels.

Shock

Your dog may go into shock as a result of a burn or an injury. If the dog is unconscious, check to be sure the airway is open. Clear secretions from the mouth with your fingers, using a piece of cloth. Pull the tip of the tongue forward beyond the front teeth to make it easier for the dog to breathe. Keep the dog's head lower than her body by placing a blanket beneath her hindquarters and using another blanket to keep the dog warm on the way to the vet's office.

If the dog is not breathing, begin artificial respiration immediately. To give a Boxer artificial respiration, follow these important steps:

1. **Place the dog on her side with her head low to the ground.**

2. **Close the dog's mouth by clasping your hand around her muzzle.**

   Be careful that you don't cause her teeth to close over her tongue.

3. **Place your mouth over the dog's nose, and blow into the dog's nostrils.**

   The chest should expand.

4. **Release your mouth to let the dog exhale.**

5. **Repeat so the dog gets 20 breaths per minute (one breath every three seconds).**

6. **Continue administering artificial respiration until the dog breathes on her own, or as long as her heart beats.**

Bites and bleeding wounds

If your Boxer is bleeding, you must attend to the wounds right away. If the flow of blood is not stemmed, your dog could bleed to death. Apply pressure directly to the bleeding point with a cotton pad or compress soaked in cold water. If the bleeding continues, seek your veterinarian's help immediately.

If your Boxer is bitten by another dog, get your dog to the veterinarian without delay. Even the most minor bite wounds can be infected and should get antibiotic treatment immediately.

Poisons

Always keep the telephone numbers of your local or national poison control center and the local 24-hour emergency veterinary hospital current and easily available. If you know or suspect what kind of poison your dog has ingested, give this information to the poison control center. They may be able to prescribe an immediate antidote. When you speak to your vet, pass on any information the poison control center gives you.

If you aren't sure whether your dog has been poisoned or do not know which poison he may have ingested, be prepared to describe the symptoms you are observing to the poison control center or your veterinarian. Common symptoms of poisoning are paralysis, convulsions, tremors, diarrhea, vomiting, and stomach cramps accompanied by howling, heavy breathing, and whimpering.

Many seemingly harmless household substances can be extremely dangerous if ingested by your dog. Antifreeze, paint thinners, chocolate, and numerous decorative plants could easily take your dog's life. Read labels and discuss potentially harmful household items with your veterinarian.

Some plants that can be harmful to your dog include the following:

- ✔ Airplane plant
- ✔ Azalea

- ✔ Caladium

- ✔ Cyclamen

- ✔ Diffenbachia

- ✔ Foxglove

- ✔ Holly

- ✔ Jerusalem cherry

- ✔ Mistletoe

- ✔ Mother-in-law's tongue

- ✔ Philodendron

- ✔ Poinsettia

- ✔ Rhododendron

- ✔ Spider plant

- ✔ Yew

Broken bones

If you suspect that your dog has broken a bone, remain calm. If you don't handle the situation correctly and immediately, injuries sustained by your Boxer can be fatal. Panic on your part can upset the animal even further and cause her to thrash about, making matters even worse.

If your Boxer is unable to stand, if one of her legs is held at an unnatural angle, or if she reacts painfully to being touched, try to obtain assistance in moving the dog. Getting help is particularly important if the dog was injured on the road. Make every effort to support the dog's body as much as possible. If a blanket or coat is available, slip this under the dog and move the injured animal by using the blanket or coat to hold the dog up.

Do not attempt to determine how serious the injuries may be. Often, broken bones may be accompanied by internal bleeding and damage that you are unable to detect. Get your dog to the veterinarian's office immediately. If someone is available to drive you and your dog to the veterinary hospital, all the better. That way, you can devote your attention to keeping the dog as calm and immobile as possible.

You can make a temporary leg splint by forming a tube around the injured Boxer's leg with a substantial section of the newspaper. Then wrap the tube with bandage or adhesive tape to keep the leg from moving.

Foreign objects and choking

All puppies and even some adult dogs have a need to pick up every little object they find on the floor or out in the yard and get it into their mouths. And these objects can often get lodged or trapped across their teeth, usually halfway back or even where the two jaws hinge. If you see your Boxer pawing at his mouth or rubbing his jaws along the ground, check to see if there is something lodged in his mouth.

If something is lodged in your dog's jaws, grasp the object between your fingers and push firmly toward the *back* of the mouth where the teeth are wider apart. This technique normally dislodges the object, but be sure to have a firm grip on the object so the dog does not swallow it after you get it loose. If the object does not come loose immediately, get your Boxer to the veterinarian right away.

If your dog appears to be gagging or choking and the object is not visible in the mouth, he may already have swallowed it. If the item is in the dog's throat, the dog may be choking. Wedge something like a screwdriver handle or similar object in the dog's jaw to keep the jaws open. Pulling the dog's tongue out should reveal any objects lodged at the back of the throat. If you see anything at the back of the throat, grasp the object firmly and pull it out. If the dog seems to be having trouble breathing, the object could be lodged in the windpipe. Sharp blows to the rib cage can help make the dog expel air from the lungs and expel the object as well.

Whenever any small object is missing in your home and you suspect your Boxer has swallowed it, do not hesitate to consult your veterinarian. X-rays can normally reveal the hidden treasure and save your dog's life.

Bloat

Gastric torsion, more commonly referred to as *bloat,* is a potentially fatal problem. Do not attempt any home remedy without your veterinarian's immediate advice.

The onset of bloat is recognizable almost immediately. The dog's abdominal area seems to blow up before your eyes as though an air hose has been inserted down his throat and turned on full blast. The skin becomes very taut and the dog becomes increasingly restless. Breathing is heavy and he is obviously extremely uncomfortable if not crying in pain. In this situation, minutes count. Get on the phone to your vet *immediately.*

Heatstroke

The body temperature of a dog suffering from heatstroke soars above the normal 100 to 102.5 degrees. The dog's breath is very rapid but shallow. If your dog is suffering from heatstroke, you need to cool the dog down immediately, either in a tub of cool water or with a garden hose. Place ice packs on the dog's abdomen, head, neck, and body. Cover the dog's body with water-cooled towels. Call your vet right away.

The easiest way for a Boxer to get heatstroke is for the dog to be left in a car in hot weather. Never leave your dog in a car, even for a few minutes.

Hypothermia

In northern climates, Boxers may also be in danger of *hypothermia,* a condition in which the dog's body temperature drops below normal — a temperature drop of just a few degrees could spell danger. When a dog is suffering from hypothermia, her heart rate increases significantly and shivering sets in. Immerse the dog in warm water or wrap the dog in warmed blankets or heating pads to bring the dog's temperature back up to normal.

If the dog's mouth and tongue begin to turn blue, this is a sign that circulation is shutting down. Warm the dog as much as possible and call your vet immediately.

Stings and bites

Stings and bites are a common cause of hives or swelling around the eyes or lip area. Boxers are forever curious and tend to give crawling and flying insects more attention than they deserve. This natural curiosity often results in potentially harmful stings and bites around the feet or, even worse, around the mouth and nose.

Visible stings can be treated with a pair of tweezers. When the stinger is removed, apply a saline solution or mild antiseptic to the site of the sting. If the swelling is large, particularly inside the mouth, or if the dog appears to be in shock, consult your veterinarian immediately.

Snake bites from poisonous snakes necessitate immediate action, because snake venom travels to the nerve centers very quickly. If your dog has been bitten by a snake, keep the dog as calm and quiet as possible. Venom spreads rapidly if the dog is more active. Excitement, exercise, and struggling increase the rate of the venom's absorption. If possible, carry the dog into your vet's office instead of letting him walk.

Do not wash the wound, because this increases the absorption of the venom into the body. Do not apply ice, because this does not slow absorption and can only serve to damage the dog's skin.

Because different snake venoms require different anti-venoms, try to get a very good look at the snake and describe it to your vet in as much detail as you can.

Porcupine quills

If your Boxer's nose has come up against the porcupine's defense system and you are unable to get your dog to a veterinarian, do your best to muzzle the dog before attempting to do anything else. Then cut the quills back to an inch or two from the skin's surface and remove them with a pair of pliers, pulling them out with a straight, forward motion. A veterinarian's attention is important, even after you've removed the quills.

Skunk

If you live in the suburbs or the country, your Boxer could easily come into contact with skunks. Your dog will probably not enjoy his encounter with a skunk, but *you* will hate it!

Even though a skunk encounter is not exactly a medical emergency, it is a situation that requires immediate action. Many commercial products sold by pet stores eliminate the odor quickly and thoroughly. If you are unable to obtain one of these products when you need it, tomato juice is a handy and effective remedy. Spray the dog thoroughly with the juice, allowing it to remain on the coat for approximately 20 minutes. Then rinse the tomato juice off the dog and, if possible, allow the dog to dry in the sun.

Odor is not the only problem resulting from an encounter with a skunk. Reports of rabid skunks are alarmingly high, and skunks are not the least bit timid about defending themselves. If skunks are present in your area or if you plan on taking your dog to an area where skunks may be found, be sure to have your Boxer's rabies shots up to date.

A Spoonful of Sugar: Getting Your Dog to Take His Medicine

Follow-up care often requires giving your dog some sort of medicine. If you think getting your 60-pound child to take his medicine is difficult, wait until you try it with your 60-pound Boxer! In the following sections, I give you a few tricks and tips that can make this job easier for everyone involved.

Applying ointments

If you have to apply an ointment to your dog's eye or ear, you'll be glad to know that nearly all of these medications come in tubes with nozzle applicators. These applicators help aim the medication exactly where you want it to go — into the eye or down the ear canal, for example. This type of tube also helps get ointments into punctures or cuts.

Muzzle your Boxer if you're applying an ointment that may sting or burn. The inside of a Boxer's ear is particularly sensitive and the application of medication there can sometimes be startling to the dog, so muzzling helps in this situation as well.

Getting your Boxer to swallow pills

Although you can use a number of methods for getting a pill down your dog's throat, I have found that the fine art of deception works best. I usually disguise the pill in a bit of my dog's favorite food or snack. Although I certainly do not recommend sugar as a mainstay in your Boxer's diet, Mary Poppins's counsel that "a spoonful of sugar helps the medicine go down" can be taken literally here. Rolling the pill up in a bit of soft candy, or better yet, some peanut butter can get the pill over the tongue and down the throat in a second, and it certainly beats trying to wrestle your friend into submission. Cheese or tuna work equally well if they are on your Boxer's top ten treats list. I usually give my dogs a pill-free sample of the food first to whet their appetite. Then I can bet that the second treat, containing the pill, will be wolfed down in a split second.

Putting medication in a dog's food dish and assuming it has been eaten is not a good idea. Many dogs have built-in pill detectors and can find a pill the size of a pinhead faster than you can say their names. These same clever detectives also know just where to hide the pill so you won't find it for at least a week or two!

If trickery or burying the pill in your dog's food doesn't work, you may have to resort to manual insertion. Do this gently and whisper sweet nothings to your dog while you do so. Simply open your dog's mouth and place the pill at the back of his tongue. Close his mouth and tilt the dog's head upwards until the pill is swallowed. To encourage swallowing, gently stroke your Boxer's throat. When you see your dog gulp, you'll know the pill is on its way to doing some good. Be sure you watch your patient for a few minutes afterward, to make sure the pill doesn't wind up on the floor. (Some dogs will do anything to avoid swallowing a pill.) Check out Figure 11-1 for illustrated instructions for giving your Boxer pills.

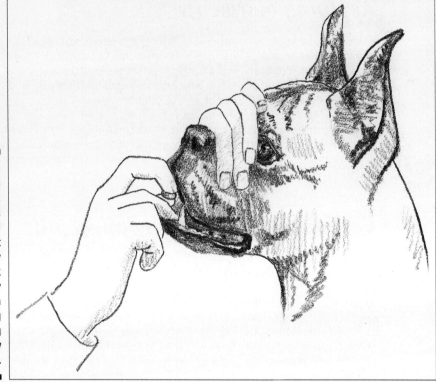

Figure 11-1:
If disguising the pill in your dog's favorite food doesn't work, try this quick and easy approach for getting your dog to swallow a pill.

Liquid medication

Trying to put a spoonful of medicine into your Boxer's mouth can be a bigger chore than you might imagine, especially if the medicine has a taste your dog dislikes. A turkey baster (or a syringe if you only have to give a small amount of liquid) can help you solve the problem easily. Shoot the medication into the side of the dog's mouth or under the tongue.

Don't shoot any liquids directly into the throat area, because the dog could easily choke. If you are giving a large dose, administer it slowly and make sure you give your dog enough time to swallow.

Chapter 12

Coping with Chronic Health Problems

In This Chapter

▶ Being aware of the chronic conditions that your Boxer may encounter in his lifetime

▶ Looking into herbal therapy and homeopathy

▶ Uncovering alternative treatments for common canine ailments

*R*esponsible Boxer breeders do everything in their power to purge their breeding stock of genetic disorders. And as a concerned buyer, you should seek out a responsible breeder, to avoid genetic disorders. However, through no one's fault, even dogs from the very best bloodlines can develop chronic health problems. And at that point, finding someone to blame isn't really a concern, because the afflicted Boxer has become a cherished part of his human family. So the owners must find a way to either correct the problem or learn how to deal with it so that the dog can enjoy a long life and live as pain-free as you possibly can make it. In this chapter, I explain how to do exactly that.

Living with Chronic Conditions

Boxers are relatively free of chronic health conditions, but as with humans, some dogs get sick. This isn't necessarily the fault of the breeder or the owner. What matters is knowing how to deal with the condition so that you can help your dog live a happy life. The following sections cover some chronic conditions that Boxers have been known to get.

Hip dysplasia

Hip dysplasia (sometimes referred to by the acronym HD) is of such a complicated genetic nature that even the most discriminating breeder has to deal with it on occasion. The problem cannot be detected in very young Boxer puppies, but as a puppy grows, particularly during the accelerated growth period that takes place between three and nine months of age, the condition begins to manifest itself. Symptoms can be so minor that they're undetectable without resorting to x-ray examination. Or the symptoms can affect the dog's movement, sometimes even crippling the dog.

If hip dysplasia is suspected, a veterinary x-ray should be conducted, with the dog anesthetized. In some cases, symptoms seem more apparent while the dog is experiencing growth and may diminish upon maturity. The degree of dysplasia and how much affects the dog will determine what must be done to keep the dog from unnecessary discomfort. Mild cases may necessitate only rest, restricting high-intensity exercise, and weight control. Serious and debilitating cases may require surgery. Only your veterinarian can make this determination, but rest assured that there are ways of coping with the disease.

Bone disorders

Many large and giant breeds, including Boxers, are susceptible to bone and joint diseases that can be traced to a nutritional, environmental, or hereditary cause. Still others are brought about by physical stress or accident.

Because these bone and joint disorders can stem from such a wide range of causes, limping or painful areas should be observed closely. If these symptoms persist, you should confine your dog and consult your veterinarian immediately. A veterinarian's diagnosis is critical, because treatment ranges from prescribed medication to physical therapy and could prevent permanent damage.

Hypothyroidism

Hypothyroidism is a condition in which the thyroid gland malfunctions and its output is reduced. This output can be adjusted and regulated by daily doses of thyroid hormone. Even with treatment, the dog will need considerable time (at least six to eight weeks) before improvement can be seen. In many cases, treatment is lifelong.

Bloat

The occurrence of bloat (technically referred to as *gastric torsion*) cannot be predicted. Unless detected at the onset of the condition and corrected by surgery, it can prove fatal. Because Boxers are susceptible to this condition, keep your Boxer from consuming large amounts of dry food in hot weather, when she is likely to then consume considerable amounts of water. A Boxer should also not be allowed to exercise strenuously for at least an hour before or after meals.

You will have no difficulty in recognizing the symptoms of this condition. The dog's abdominal area blows up as though an air hose has been inserted down his throat and turned on full blast. The affected dog's skin becomes very taut and the dog becomes increasingly restless. Breathing becomes very rapid and he is obviously extremely uncomfortable and in pain. If you suspect that your dog may have bloat, get her to a veterinarian immediately. The condition is life-threatening when untreated.

Aortic stenosis and cardiomyopathy

Both aortic stenosis and cardiomyopathy are conditions that involve the heart and they must be carefully supervised and treated by an experienced veterinarian. Neither of these conditions can be prevented, but some of the complications can be medically alleviated.

Research in other breeds with congenital heart problems may indicate that neglecting dental hygiene can exacerbate heart conditions.

Cancerous and benign tumors

Skin tumors are common in Boxers, but a vast percentage of them are benign. Benign tumors appear at random on the body. They increase in size within themselves. In some cases where rapid growth is anticipated, benign tumors should be removed surgically.

Cancerous tumors can spread into adjacent areas of the body or may release cells to form secondary tumors in other organs. Possible treatment includes removal through surgery, chemotherapy, and radiotherapy.

Conjunctivitis

Airborne debris such as pollen and dust, smoke, and bacteria can create an inflammation of the membrane that covers the inner surface of your Boxer's eyelid. The condition causes inflammation and tearing and, in advanced cases, a sensitivity to light. Conjunctivitis can normally be cleared up by removing the airborne cause of the infection and medicating the eye itself. One type of conjunctivitis, called *follicular conjunctivitis,* can be resistant to medication and may require surgery.

Skin disorders

Just as in bone disorders, the causes of skin disorders can run the gamut. Tumors, hereditary allergies, infections, parasites, and hormonal imbalances can all cause skin disorders. Extensive research into all of these areas has been done, and although control can at times be lengthy and costly, advances are made each year in this area. Treatments are available to relieve your Boxer's suffering in some cases. Other skin disorders run rampant, with no hope of a cure.

Usually, when your Boxer starts scratching, that's a good sign that he may have a skin disorder. Within days, the dog may scratch so often and so severely that parts of his coat will be scratched away. Always check the skin in the area that is being scratched and in the areas that are harder for the dog to reach as well.

Any signs of skin eruptions, puffiness, or irritation should be cause for concern. Some dogs are extremely sensitive to fleas, and at the first flea bite the dog will begin scratching so furiously that the skin will be damaged, bringing about the onset of *chronic flea dermatitis*. If your Boxer has this extreme sensitivity, being especially diligent about keeping your home and property free of fleas is absolutely essential. Your veterinarian will be able to recommend the products best suited to the flea-sensitive Boxer.

Aging changes the quality and texture of the dog's skin. The aging dog's skin is far more sensitive to attacks from fleas, lice, and ticks. Be even more judicious about keeping your older Boxer's coat clean and well brushed. Your veterinarian may recommend a change in diet or diet supplements to help keep your older dog's skin and coat healthy.

Taking a Look at Herbs and Homeopathy

Our interest in a natural way to maintain health through diet and exercise has naturally been accompanied by a fascination with nature's own way to restore fading health with natural remedies. A realization that many of modern science's drugs are derivatives or chemical simulations of plants and herbs found in nature created interest in the fields known as herbalist and homeopathic medicine.

Herbal therapy

Conventional medicine is not the only way to ward off chronic problems. Natural medication, as practiced by the Chinese for many centuries and in many cases by our own grandparents, has been found to have many healing properties. And in a good many cases, natural medication has fewer side effects than artificially created medications do.

Herbs growing in nature have been used effectively for centuries and are now the basis for what is popularly referred to as *herbal therapy.* Scientific research has revealed that there is certainly no mystery involved in herbs' effectiveness. *When properly prescribed and administered,* no risk is involved in taking them.

Most herbal remedies are obtainable over the counter without prescription. Because they are so easily attainable and in many cases so effective, a logical but false assumption is that what works for humans will also work for our dogs. But this is not always the case. In fact, assuming that what works for you will work for your Boxer could prove fatal for your dog. Even though your Boxer may be suffering from the same or a similar malady as you, the canine system operates much differently than a human's.

If you have found herbal remedies effective for yourself and want to consider this alternative approach for your dog, be sure to consult a trained and experienced herbalist. Be careful though. Your local herbalist is most likely *not* a veterinarian. More and more veterinarians are using herbal remedies in their practices, but if you can't find a veterinarian who does, I strongly suggest that you consider working with an herbalist and a veterinarian in tandem. The herbalist will be able to suggest what works best, and your veterinarian can determine whether the herb is safe for canines.

If your Boxer is already on a prescription medication, your veterinarian's scientific knowledge can assist you in deciding whether you can safely use the herbal recommendation and the prescription medication together. If you determine that the two recommended medications do not or will not work together safely, you need to decide which approach to use — the traditional medicine or the herbal one. Most vets are willing to work along with an herbalist.

If your Boxer has been under treatment with a veterinarian who does not feel comfortable in approving the use of herbs, you need to decide whether to follow your vet's recommendation or get a second opinion from another vet. Only you can make this call.

More and more reports are being published that highlight the successful use of herbal therapy in treating chronic skin conditions that have been totally resistant to all other approaches. Owners whose dogs are suffering from rheumatoid arthritis report significant results through herbal therapy. Changes in diet and the use of natural nutritional supplements are proving to reverse the arthritic condition and are allowing dogs to return to the natural flexibility and athleticism of their younger days. Recent studies have also revealed that some herbs offer marked help in improving a dog's memory, in scent work, and in reducing stress. Herbs are also being credited for improving dogs' general health and well-being.

Because no regulatory controls are placed on herbs and herbal remedies, strengths and required dosages vary from one product to the next. Be extremely careful when giving your dog herbal remedies, and never administer any herbal treatment that does not have the product's strength clearly printed on the container.

Herbal teas are excellent for dogs because they are quickly and easily assimilated into the system. You can add herbal tea to your dog's food or, in some cases, to your dog's drinking water.

Homeopathy

Although homeopathy may appear to be a product of New Age thought, it is far from being new. The roots of homeopathy go back as far as the ancient Greeks, but Dr. Samuel Hahnemann (1755–1843) is credited as the father of the homeopathic approach to health care. Medical practices during Dr. Hahnemann's time were absolutely barbaric, with cutting, hacking, bloodletting, and violent poisons and *emetics* (vomit-inducing substances) resorted to even when the patient was doing all he or she could to cling to life.

Medicine in those early days dealt solely with the symptoms of a disease. Even if the patient survived the often savage treatment of those symptoms, the cause remained untreated and reoccurrence was almost assured. Dr. Hahnemann believed that the symptoms were simply a sign that something was not working properly within the person's system. He set about trying to find a more civilized approach to dealing with the symptoms by seeking the source of the problem.

Hahnemann also felt that the best healer was the person's own system, or, as it is referred to in homeopathic circles, the person's *vital force*. Dr. Hahnemann believed that if he could encourage the system itself to deal with the intruding problem, a permanent cure would happen naturally.

To better understand how homeopathic medicine differs from conventional *(allopathic)* medicine we can use a Boxer's skin rash as an example. The homeopathic approach would consider the dog's skin rash as a manifestation (or a symptom) of his vital force doing battle with a problem on a much deeper level. Thus, finding the internal cause and treating it would be the homeopathic practitioner's approach. The conventional, or *allopathic,* practitioner would determine what kind of rash the dog was suffering from and prescribe treatment to eliminate the rash. If the prescribed ointment or pill did not eliminate the rash, tests would be conducted to determine what external substances were causing the rash. Attempts would then be made to eliminate the substance from the dog's environment.

These two approaches do not necessarily conflict, however. In fact, the two move closer together as the years pass and as modern medicine more fully understands the value of the holistic approach. In the future, both views will undoubtedly be able to modify and assist each other in bringing about what is referred to as *complementary medicine,* thereby creating even greater medical advances.

Several organizations devoted to holistic veterinary medicine can provide you with more information. They can also help you find a practitioner in your area. Here are five of the best holistic organizations geared specifically toward animals:

- **Academy of Veterinary Homeopathy,** telephone: 305-652-1590

- **American Holistic Veterinary Medical Association,** telephone: 410-569-0795

- **American Veterinary Chiropractic Association,** telephone: 309-658-2920

- **International Association for Veterinary Homeopathy,** telephone: 770-516-5954

- **International Veterinary Acupuncture Society,** telephone: 303-682-1167

Be very careful in seeking out a homeopathic practitioner. Anyone can call himself a homeopath. Not everyone, however, can call themselves *homeopathic veterinarians.* To call oneself a veterinarian of any kind at all, the person must have a degree in veterinary medicine — Doctor of Veterinary Medicine (DVM) or Veterinary Medical Doctor (VMD).

Exploring Other Alternative Treatments for Your Boxer

Acupuncture, acupressure, chiropractic, meridian therapy, and massage for dogs? Am I serious? You betcha! These therapies are becoming increasingly popular with pet owners, and more and more practitioners are available across the country. If old Dr. Hahnemann was correct (see the preceding section) and our systems are regulated by a vital force, it would follow that we have to keep that force flowing to all parts of the body, right? Of course! And that is exactly what *body work therapies* are all about — keeping the channels open so the force can be with us (or our dogs) in every little nook and cranny of our bodies.

Acupuncture and acupressure

The ancient Chinese practice of acupuncture and acupressure are proven methods of relieving pain and eliminating chronic conditions. These treatments work through the use of very thin needles or the fingers to stimulate specific points of the body. Modern science has found that the needles or pressure applied help release corrective substances within the system and also help realign the system's natural energy flows. When the channels are open, the corrective substances are able to reach the injured or ailing points.

Chiropractic medicine

Chiropractic medicine is another alternative approach to injury relief that has been effectively used on human patients for many years. But only recently has it been found to be an effective and valuable tool in veterinary medicine. In chiropractic therapy, the studied manipulation of joints, bones, and the surrounding tissues results in releasing energy flows through the nerves and spinal cord to the affected areas.

Massage

Many people believe that dogs take on a great deal of their owners' tension. This in turn creates stress for the dogs and leads to abnormal tightness, which makes the dog more prone to injuries.

Massage therapy is aimed at relieving tension in your dog's muscles and soft tissues. Those who practice holistic medicine believe massage therapy assists in balancing, channeling natural energy. Massage is particularly useful in the treatment of circulatory and neurological problems as well as in joint and spine disorders.

Massage, acupuncture, and acupressure all have the same goal — releasing the flow of blocked energy to allow the body itself to correct a condition. Therefore, it is not uncommon for a holistic practitioner to employ all three of these approaches to better health.

Unfortunately, finding a professional practitioner qualified to treat your Boxer may not be easy. Currently, there are no official organizations for animal massage and acupuncture. There are, however, organizations that teach these techniques. Equine and Canine Acupressure of Parker, Colorado, conducts classes nation-wide. They can be contacted by e-mail at equineacup@earthlink.net or by telephone at 303-722-1117 or toll-free at 888-841-7211.

Canine Massage Awareness offers a home study course. The Web site of this organization based in Ontario, Canada, is www.cyberus.ca/~ema-cma. You can also contact them by telephone at 613-737-9846.

Boxers are extremely sociable dogs. After they announce the arrival of a friendly stranger, they more often than not are at the head of the receiving line to greet the new guest.

A Boxer puppy is a little dynamo of energy, but he needs many opportunities to rest throughout the day. Although Boxer puppies may seem capable of playing rough-and-tumble games for hours on end, they should never be pushed past their limits.

Small meals several times a day are important for the growing Boxer puppy. Responsible breeders always send a puppy to her new home with a diet sheet that clearly outlines the amount and brand of food the puppy is accustomed to eating.

Two Boxers can be more fun than one, but you're usually better off waiting to get the second dog until your first one has been trained and has adapted to your family's lifestyle. At that point, your adult Boxer will prove to be an asset in training the newcomer.

Never underestimate the ability of a Boxer puppy to get into places where he doesn't belong. In fact, those forbidden areas always seem to have the greatest appeal to the little explorers. Puppyproofing your home is one of the major steps in preparing for your dog's arrival.

Boxers play with toys from puppyhood through old age. Be sure to look for toys that are durable, because every toy a Boxer has will be given a very thorough endurance and destructibility test.

The first step in leash-training your Boxer puppy is having her become accustomed to a soft buckle collar. After a few scratches, most puppies forget the collar is even there.

Most Boxers learn to enjoy bath time. Be sure to place a mat on the bottom of the bathtub to provide secure footing. Boxers are more apt to fear slipping in the tub than they fear the bath itself.

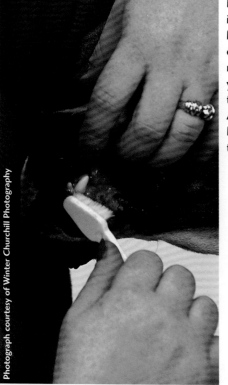

Brushing a Boxer's teeth is as important to his oral hygiene as brushing your own teeth is to yours. Use roughly the same technique you would use in brushing the teeth of a young child. And be sure to brush your Boxer's teeth no less than three or four times a week.

Clipping your Boxer's nails is an important part of her grooming, because short nails help keep the dog's feet compact and strong. Trim each nail just a little bit at a time so that you don't hurt your Boxer by cutting into the quick and causing the nail to bleed.

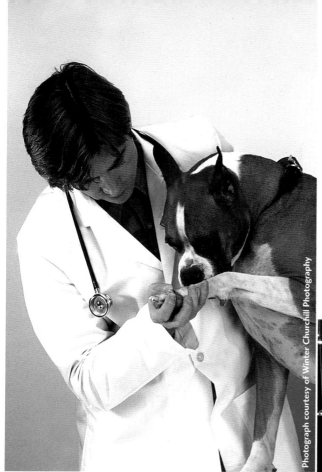

Regular veterinary checkups keep your Boxer healthy and avoid the onset of complicated problems that could prove to be very costly down the road.

Never leave home without making sure your Boxer is confined to a safe and secure place. Well-fenced, escape-proof outdoor runs with adequate shelters are best when weather permits, but if your Boxer is indoors while you are gone, his crate or cage is the safest place for him to be.

Boxers love children, and they often appoint themselves the official bodyguards of the youngest members of their household. Although a Boxer is exceptionally tolerant, children should be taught never to abuse their Boxer's instinctive kindness.

Basic obedience lessons should be a part of every young Boxer's education. Sit, down, stay, come, and heel are the five basic obedience commands that every Boxer should respond to without question.

This Boxer is well along the way in learning how to heel. On command, he will walk with his head next to his owner's left leg and will do so regardless of which direction his owner travels.

The sit and stay lesson begins with the trainer moving just a foot or two away at first. The distance is gradually increased so that, eventually, the dog will remain in position even when his trainer is completely out of sight.

A healthy, well-exercised Boxer is muscular and alert. You should just be able to feel your Boxer's ribs through a layer of resilient flesh. Do not allow your Boxer to become overweight even as a youngster, because this problem will be even more severe as she reaches old age.

Obedience lessons can be as simple as learning the five basic commands, or they can be extended to an advanced level, where a dog can earn formal obedience degrees. Boxers are particularly well-suited to these advanced courses, because they have both the desire and the athleticism necessary to perform well.

Historically, the preferred style of presenting a Boxer in the show ring and the way most Americans are accustomed to seeing the breed calls for cropped ears. But ear cropping is not necessary if the dog will never be shown. This young Boxer has what are referred to as *natural* ears.

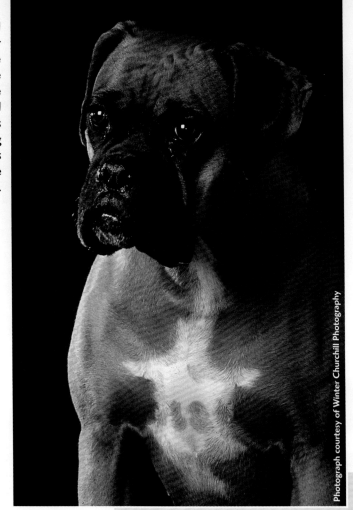

Cropped ears create a look of heightened awareness in a dog. The original purpose of the Boxer was to serve as a guard and watch dog, and the cropped ear enhanced the necessary image.

Dogs who have white markings on the head and a white collar and chest are referred to as *flashy* by Boxer fanciers. Show dogs are not required to have this coloring, but flashy Boxers are prized by some, because their appearance is very eye-catching.

Part V
The Part of Tens

The 5th Wave   By Rich Tennant

"Okay, let's get into something a little more theoretical."

In this part . . .

This is the place to turn if you want a lot of information but only have a few minutes to spare. Here you can find reasons to get a Boxer, ways to train your new friend, tips on traveling with your dog, and ways to have fun with your Boxer.

Chapter 13

Ten Reasons to Get a Boxer

In This Chapter

▶ Remembering all the traits that set a Boxer apart

▶ Taking a look at some great reasons to make a Boxer part of your family

*I*f you're not quite sure whether a Boxer is for you, this chapter provides ten great reasons to make a Boxer your new best friend.

Boxers Are Handsome

Very early on in my search for Boxer knowledge, I came upon, *The Boxer,* the book that Dr. Dan Gordon had written on the breed early in the 1950s. I will never forget the manner in which he described the breed. I still have the book — a cherished possession — so I can quote exactly what he said:

> "The really typical boxer reminds me of those few 'he men' who have climbed to the heights of adulation in the movies. Have you noticed the fact that most of these are not really 'beautiful' — are often actually almost homely if dissected — but all are rugged and masculine in appearance. That's our real boxer."

That description has remained with me through all these years. It so typifies what this wonderful breed can and should be all about. There is nothing fussy or cute in the fully matured Boxer. Handsome? Yes. Striking? Indeed. Imposing? Without a doubt!

And yes, all these attempts to characterize what a Boxer is are just as descriptive of the female side of the breed as they are of the boys. We who are immersed in the breed are probably apt to see a top-quality female and effuse, "Isn't she beautiful!" But think about it for a minute, a Standard Poodle, coiffed from head to heel is beautiful. A female Boxer — fully matured and conditioned to the height of her potential — is, without a doubt, striking and imposing and yes, even handsome.

Boxers Are Clever

And wow, are Boxers smart! I don't say that to imply that Boxers are the only dogs who can learn to sit and stay or run up to your closet and fetch your slippers. No, there are a lot of breeds more than capable of doing those jobs just as well. What I'm talking about here is just how quickly a Boxer (and particularly a Boxer girl — it takes the boys a bit longer to get there) can figure us humans out.

In short order, your Boxer will determine just what makes you laugh, what makes you angry, and just how far she can go without getting you *really* angry. A Boxer also quickly learns just which of her whole repertoire of little mannerisms can soften your determined stance and convince you that just one more little piece of cake wouldn't hurt you or her.

You are going to have to be on your toes for this breed. A Boxer can have you perfectly trained in no time at all.

Boxers Are Versatile

I have come across very few things other breeds are capable of learning that a Boxer can't do. A Boxer's talents run the whole gamut of accomplishments: guard dog, baby sitter, therapy dog, guide dog for the blind. He can be a star in the obedience ring, a whiz at agility competition, and superstar in the dog show conformation ring.

A Boxer can play a play a rough-and-tumble game of football with your teenagers one minute and gently assist the baby of the family in taking her first steps the next. The same Boxer that staunchly defends home and hearth from an intruder — with his life if he has to — is the same dog who endures his little mistress dressing him up in a bonnet and ruffled apron to join her and her friends for a tea party. He's Dad's jogging companion, Mom's food taster, and big sister's companion on a walk in the park. He can do it all!

Boxers Are Clean

Boxers housebreak in a snap. Any adult Boxer I've owned would knock down a wall before she would relieve herself in the house. The breed is clean, and every Boxer I know likes to stay that way.

It's not that a Boxer is prissy — not by a long shot. A Boxer can dig a hole to China (or at least try!) and love doing it. But when she eventually gets to the land of chopsticks, she'll come up for air, shake herself off and *voilá!* Clean as a whistle (well, almost!).

The Boxer's coat is wash and wear. A thorough brushing once or twice a week along with a good wipe down with a chamois cloth and your Boxer is clean and odor-free. Even the Boxer with white markings can be ready for a Saturday night date in a flash with a washcloth moistened with a little cleanser made especially for that purpose.

A bath, though rarely needed, will have your girl smelling like a rose and she will love you for it. (You may not want your 60-pound male to smell like a rose, so there are some ready-made masculine scents for the boys, too.)

Boxers Have a Joie de Vivre

No breed I have ever owned has a lust for life as does the Boxer. A Boxer wakes up every morning of his life with an attitude that shouts, "Hooray, it's a new day!" I have always said that every day is the Fourth of July for a Boxer — just cause for celebration.

It will take all the strength you can muster to keep a straight face when your little friend coquettishly breaks every rule in the book or when your young bull blunders happily through the petunias to greet you. But persevere you must, or else you'll find you have the canine version of Jim Carrey, Robin Williams, and Adam Sandler all rolled up into one — and then you'll learn what "over the top" really means!

Some breeds have that delightful attitude as puppies, but as they mature they settle down into being whatever it is their breed is intended to be — and that can be very dull. A Boxer is a puppy forever. Your Boxer will play with his toys until he's old and gray. And he will enjoy playing with those toys as a senior citizen as much as he did when he first came to your home as a rollicking 8-week-old pup. The Boxer is a born clown and loves to entertain the troops.

You can't stay depressed for very long with a Boxer in your home. When they were passing out the melancholy gene, Boxers were out somewhere else — thinking up a new game, I'm sure.

Boxers Are Sensitive

But just because a Boxer takes joy in living, don't think the breed is mindless. Few breeds are more attuned to their loved ones' emotions and state of being than Boxers are. If a Boxer realizes that her antics aren't appropriate or you need some downtime, she'll be more than happy to cuddle up on the sofa with you and help you think about the good old days.

Although we've been fortunate never to have had to put our Boxers to the test, friends of ours who have owned Boxers have related stories about how vigilant their dogs became when someone in the household was ill. One family's Boxer was totally distraught when his young master had seriously injured his back playing football and was confined to his bed for a considerable period of time. The dog, who was normally a happy-go-lucky, over-the-top, silly extrovert, sat for hours with his chin resting on the edge of his young master's bed, gazing at his friend for weeks on end. The day his pal was allowed up for the first time, the Boxer went back to his goofy ways and spent just as much time being as silly as only Boxers can be.

Boxers Are Reliable

Historically, the Boxer has been a breed to rely upon. Although a kaleidoscope of characteristics go into making the total Boxer, in the end he is basically a pretty reliable fellow. This breed is not one that you have to worry over which side of the bed he gets up on. He isn't going to fly off the handle "just because," nor is he the kind of dog who believes there's nothing better than the other side of the mountain. By and large, Boxers like their homes and their families and they're more than content being there.

I think a good part of that homebody temperament has been cherished and perpetuated by those who have bred Boxers over the years. Reliable people seem to like reliable dogs, and Boxers are a breed in which you can find a good many breeders who have been with the breed over the long haul. They've seen the breed experience high spots on the popularity polls and they've been there when the breed was all but forgotten.

If you get your Boxer pal from one of the breeders who has stood by the breed and continued to produce mentally and physically sound dogs through the years, you can be reasonably sure the dog you get will be just as reliable as the source from which he came.

Boxers Are Brave

There's no doubt about it: The Boxer is a brave dog and he has the physical wherewithal to back himself up. Don't forget that Boxers have achieved canine hero status as war dogs for practically every country in which they have served. And this has been the case since the breed's earliest days in Germany.

Today, the offspring of a dog who has not attained a Schutzhund title are inel-igible for registration with the Boxer Club of Germany. The word *Schutzhund* simply means "protection dog" in German, and the Boxer excels as a Schutzhund dog. A dog has to be trainable, fast, agile, and sound of mind in order to adapt to the Schutzhund training and succeed through the complex program. Time and time again, the Boxer has proven just how suitable he is for this work.

Boxers Are Charismatic

The Boxer is undoubtedly one of the flashiest and most eye-catching Working Dogs shown in the conformation rings all over the world. Boxers have achieved the supreme Best In Show award at the most prestigious events held in the United States and abroad. They have done exceedingly well at New York's famed Westminster Kennel Club dog show, and three Boxers have scaled the heights there by winning the coveted Best In Show award.

Boxers Are International

The Boxer has admirers all over the world. There's not a dog showing country anywhere that doesn't have a respectable Boxer representation. Boxer breed-ers, exhibitors, and just plain Boxer-lovers from around the world now com-municate daily on Internet chat rooms. The online Boxer-lovers discuss health issues, breeding, and training problems, and swap good old-fashioned dog sto-ries. Which reminds me, did I ever tell you about the time good old Rocky. . . .

Chapter 14

Ten Great Training Tips

In This Chapter

▶ Knowing your role in your Boxer's life

▶ Getting tips on training your dog to be the best pal he can be

▶ Being kind and consistent with your Boxer

*T*raining your Boxer isn't about imposing your will on your otherwise cheerful and rambunctious pal. It's about building a relationship with your dog and letting him know that you're there for him, protecting him and watching out for him no matter what. A well-trained dog is happier, because he has more freedom than an untamed beast. When you've trained your Boxer well, he'll be a great companion with you, wherever you go. In this chapter, I provide some basic training tips, things to keep in mind as you train your dog, from puppyhood on.

Remember Your Role

As the owner of a Boxer — or of any dog, for that matter — your role is to serve as your dog's leader. Dogs are pack animals, and puppies who have just left the comfort of their mother and littermates will look to you to fill that empty space. So your job is not only to comfort and protect your dog, but also to teach him the rules. When your puppy knows what's expected of him, you'll both be happier.

A leader isn't a dictator. You don't have to be cruel or harsh to be a good leader. Boxers are extremely sensitive dogs, and they want nothing more than to please you. So train your dog using kindness rather than punishment. You'll get the behavior you want without damaging your relationship with your Boxer in the process.

Figure Out How to Communicate with Your Boxer

Dogs communicate . . . they just do it differently than humans do. And your job is to figure out what your dog is trying to tell you.

Be able to recognize the difference between active and passive behavior. A dog who is exhibiting active behavior tends to move in a forward and up direction (whereas the passive dog moves backward and down). If your Boxer is challenging authority, she may step forward with stiff legs. The hair on the back of her neck and shoulders may be standing up. She holds her head up and looks straight ahead, staring at the person she views as a threat. Her teeth are clenched and she may growl. A dog who is passive, on the other hand, lowers his head with his ears pinned back. If you approach a passive dog, he may roll over onto his back with his legs in the air.

If your dog is exhibiting aggressive behavior toward you, be sure to talk with your breeder and/or veterinarian. Aggressive behavior isn't acceptable in a Boxer. Try to determine what has triggered your dog's response before you respond.

Punish Your Dog Appropriately

Punishment has its place in the world of training. But too often, people punish their dogs when it's too late. If you walk into your living room to find your puppy has taken care of his business all over your brand new carpeting, yelling at or scolding your dog after the fact will do nothing. The accident may have happened minutes or even hours ago. And your puppy won't associate the punishment you're delivering after the fact with the accident he had earlier. In order for punishment to be effective, you have to deliver it immediately after the negative behavior takes place.

Punishment should *never* involve abuse. Hitting, kicking, or otherwise injuring your dog does nothing but build a wall between you and teach your dog that violence is okay. If you have trouble controlling your temper, perhaps a dog just isn't for you.

Use Positive Reinforcement

Getting frustrated with a rambunctious young pup is natural. But many dog owners, in their efforts to train their dogs, tend to punish bad behavior and forget to reward good behavior. Punishing bad behavior has its benefits when it's done appropriately (see the previous section for more on using punishment wisely). But rewarding good behavior is always a positive thing.

When your dog learns that doing what you ask gets her a new chew toy or a treat (or even just lots of verbal praise), she'll aim to please you every time. And unlike punishment, which the dog may not understand, your Boxer will quickly associate the reward with the behavior you're looking for.

Use Your Dog's Name with Every Command

Whenever you ask your dog to do something, precede the command with her name — "Daisy, come," "Daisy, sit," or "Daisy, down," for example. Using your dog's name like this not only helps her recognize her name sooner, it also ensures that you'll always be able to get her attention when you need it.

Manage Your Dog So That He Can't Get into Trouble in the First Place

Part of successfully training a dog is doing your part as your dog's owner. If your dog gets into the trash and finds a discarded piece of food, you'll have a much tougher time convincing him that digging in the trash isn't rewarding than if you never allowed him to get into the trash in the first place.

Too often, well-intentioned dog owners forget that dogs need to be kept out of trouble just like children do. Walk around your house and look at everything from your dog's perspective. Will clothes lying on the floor seem like toys to your dog? Probably. Will your puppy try pulling on the low-hanging tablecloth just for the fun of it? You can bet on it. You can't completely prevent your puppy from getting into trouble (after all, that's what puppies were made to do), but you can try your best to move items that are off-limits out of his reach.

Find a Good Trainer for Your Dog

You can do a lot of training on your own with your dog. And you should never expect a trainer to replace your own training. But a good trainer can help you and your dog reach a new level of obedience.

Always look for a trainer who has had years of experience and can provide solid references. And steer clear of anyone who promises results overnight.

Know When Your Dog May Need Extra Help

Some dogs, just like some people, have emotional problems that prevent them from learning as quickly as you'd like. Your dog may be suffering from separation anxiety, for example. And yelling at him for chewing up the newspaper while you're away doesn't do any good. Instead, you need to figure out what the source of the problem is and figure out how to help your dog overcome it.

If your Boxer is exhibiting a behavior problem that you think is more than just a little misbehaving, consult your breeder first. An experienced breeder can suggest someone who can help you through your situation. Talk to your veterinarian as well. Behavior specialists are available to deal with particularly troubled dogs, and your vet may be able to refer you to someone in your area.

Never hit or harm a dog who is acting out. That may only make the emotional problems worse.

Be Consistent

Part of being a leader is being consistent with the rules. Training a puppy is no different than having a child in this respect. If you told your teenager that her curfew was midnight, and you only grounded her for staying out late every once in a while, she'd eventually realize you weren't serious. The same holds true for your Boxer.

If you're going to set rules for your dog (which you most definitely should), you have to be prepared to enforce them every single time they're broken. And that means that if you're not around to enforce the rules, you have to be sure that your dog isn't able to break them. Confine the dog to an area where he can't get into trouble. Otherwise, just like a teenager, your Boxer will learn that he can get away with murder when you're not home.

Be Patient

I've saved the most important tip for last. Remember that your dog is very intelligent. But he only knows what you teach him — or what he learns on his own. And what dogs learn on their own are often not the lessons we want them to learn. So it's your job to teach your dog the rules, with love and patience. Even though you may have trouble remembering this when your puppy knocks over the trash can or chews everything in sight, he really wants to please you. Be patient, and he'll turn out to be one of your best friends.

Chapter 15

Ten Tips for Traveling with (and without) Your Boxer

*W*hen you plan your next trip — whether it's to the grocery store or across the country — the question of whether your Boxer should hop in the back seat is not as simple as it seems. Taking your dog along when you shop, go out of town on a business trip, or travel on vacation involves some forethought. And the longer you plan to be away, the more preparation you need to do. In this chapter, I give you ten great tips for traveling — with or without your Boxer.

Make Your Car Safe for Your Dog

Before you put your Boxer in your car and head out on the road, think about the space your car offers and what else you will be transporting. If you're carrying valuables with you, consider the safety of both your possessions *and* your dog. The larger the car, the safer your pal will be. SUVs and minivans are extremely popular and are actually far more useful to you and your Boxer than a passenger car. If you have access to one of these vehicles, take advantage of it!

If you have a Boxer and you're also in the market for a new car, try to find one that's large enough to accommodate your family *and* your full-grown dog. Tiny red sports cars may be on your mind, but they don't offer much room for your Boxer.

Your Boxer really doesn't care what size your car is, just as long as he can ride along in it. You're responsible for making sure that both your canine companion and whatever else you are toting along arrive at your destination safe and sound. Although you may not have the space that a minivan provides, all cars have trunks, and that is where *all* loose objects should be stashed while you travel. When your Boxer is secured by a car seat belt and when any other potentially flying object is safely locked up in the trunk, you can concentrate on driving safely and enjoying your trip.

Be Sure Your Dog Is Always Warm or Cool Enough

One of the most important factors in traveling with a dog is making sure that she's able to maintain the correct body temperature while she travels. Whether that means keeping her warm in the winter or cool in the summer, you're responsible for the job.

Although most people don't think of temperatures in the 80s as unbearable, on a sunny day the temperature inside a car (even one with the windows partially rolled down) can soar up over 100 degrees in just a few minutes and over 120 degrees in about 20 minutes. No dog is able to sustain these temperatures without suffering permanent brain damage or death. Never leave your dog in a car on warm, sunny days!

Be sure that if you're planning to stop along the way during hot weather, your Boxer will be able to accompany you indoors or to a shaded spot. You may find that those gourmet restaurants you are accustomed to dining in along the way will have to be relinquished for drive–thru ones, so that you can keep the air-conditioning going for your Boxer.

Buckle Up Your Boxer for Safety

Although having your dog loose, sitting right next to you in the front seat, may be nice, he could be thrown against the windshield in a sudden stop or collision, severely injuring if not killing him. And no matter how well behaved your Boxer is, if he were to spot the dog of his dreams through the driver's side window, he could leap onto your lap, impeding your vision and potentially causing an accident. The last thing you want to have to do is try to wrestle a 60-pound dog while you're doing 60 mph on the interstate.

All the reasons we humans are given for buckling up with seat belts when we drive apply to our pets as well. Canine seat belts, which can be adapted to almost any car and any dog, are now available. These special canine seat belts provide both the safety and restraint that can keep both you and your pet comfortable and safe on your trip.

A dog is safest when confined to the rear seat of a passenger car or behind a barrier in a van or SUV. Whether with seat belts or in a crate, all dogs should be restrained for their own safety. Even though riding in a solid crate may rob your dog of the opportunity to see all the sights as you travel, it's better than being hurled out of the back seat if the car stops suddenly. Try using a collapsible wire crate that can be firmly secured. This way your dog can see the sights and still travel safely.

When you hit country roads, you'll probably see ranch and farm dogs in the back of pickup trucks. Nothing could be more dangerous! A sudden stop could send the dog catapulting through the air. And even if the dog is tied down, the sudden stop could easily break the dog's neck.

Don't Forget Your Boxer's ID

Most states in the U.S. require up-to-date vaccination against rabies. If you're crossing the border to Canada or Mexico, you'll also need health certificates validated by your veterinarian. Be sure your dog's rabies inoculations are current and that your Boxer is wearing the tag your veterinarian issues indicating so.

Talk with your vet about any special precautions you may have to take, depending upon the area you are traveling to. Certain sections of the country offer higher risk of tick-borne Lyme disease and heartworm.

A collar with identification tags is an excellent way for someone to put you and your Boxer back together if you become separated. But what if the collar comes loose? Tracing you then becomes impossible.

A surefire method of positive identification that will not become separated from your dog is the *microchip*. A microchip is about the size of a grain of rice and has an unalterable code on it that can be easily read by a scanner. The chip is inserted under the dog's skin between the shoulders with a syringe by a veterinarian. The chip is totally inert and is encased in bio-compatible glass; it has proven harmless to animals of all kinds.

After the microchip has been inserted, the animal can be registered with the AKC Companion Animal Recovery program for a one-time fee of $12.50, which enrolls the animal for life. When the pet is found and turned in to an animal shelter or veterinarian, the first order of business is to scan the animal to see whether she is carrying a chip. Scanners are becoming standard equipment in most shelters and veterinary offices around the country.

If the pet carries a chip, the AKC's toll-free number is called and a Companion Animal Recovery representative notifies the owner that his pet has been found and tells the owner where the animal is being held. The AKC also calls back the vet or shelter to let them know the owner has been contacted.

Schering-Plough Animal Health is the organization that distributes the microchip under the name "Home Again" and the AKC provides database management services for a national recovery program. Your own vet can give you more information about "Home Again," or you can contact the organization directly at 800-566-3596. AKC Companion Animal Recovery can provide information as well by phone at 800-252-7894 or by fax at 919-233-1290.

Bring Supplies for Your Dog's Journey

If you plan ahead, even the longest trip with your Boxer can be a totally pleasant experience. Think about the dog supplies you use at home, and use that list as your guide for on-the-road travel.

Professional dog show handlers are on the road a good part of every week. Experience has taught them to carry everything their dogs may need both as a matter of daily routine and in case of an emergency. Your traveling companion probably has no need for all the cosmetic equipment that a show dog requires, but a number of doggie items should definitely be stowed in your Boxer's suitcase:

- **Sufficient food for the length of the trip plus a little bit more, in case your trip is extended unexpectedly.** Changing food suddenly can cause diarrhea.

- **An ice chest with refreezable ice packs.** Ice packs are a wonderful way to cool down your dog if he gets too hot. Just wrap the ice packs in a towel and place them in the bottom of your dog's travel crate in extremely hot weather.

- **Regular drinking water in one-gallon plastic containers.**

- **A brush and comb.**

- **Grooming supplies, including nail clippers and a toothbrush.**

- **A collar with clearly marked ID and rabies tags, and a leash.**

- **A canine first aid kit.** See Chapter 11 for more information on what to include in your kit.

- **A solid or collapsible crate.**

- **A list of parks and/or rest stops along the way.**

- **A pooper-scooper and plastic grocery bags.** When you're on the road, you're still responsible for picking up after your dog.

✔ Bedding that's appropriate for the season of the year in which you're traveling.

✔ Food and water dishes.

✔ Your Boxer's favorite toys.

✔ Your dog's current medications, including flea and tick controls and heartworm preventives.

✔ Paper and terrycloth towels for cleanup and drying.

Find Dog-Friendly Lodging

Not all the hotels and motels you are accustomed to stopping at accept dogs. Even though you may not be the type of person who likes to have their travel plans so structured that every stop is reserved ahead of time, if you're traveling with your Boxer, planning your itinerary like this is something to consider. Driving until you are totally exhausted and then starting a search for dog-friendly accommodations may be an option, but it certainly isn't a very attractive one.

Call the hotel or motel you're planning to stay at before you leave on your trip, to be sure they allow dogs. Even though some establishments advertise the fact that they accept dogs, this may mean only small dogs. Or they may require all dogs to be confined outside the rooms in their own travel crates.

The Automobile Club of America publishes annually updated catalogs listing accommodations across the nation, and most indicate whether they accept dogs. Travel agents are also able to secure reserved bookings and will be able to find accommodations that will accept your Boxer.

If you will be spending time in a specific city or town, the local Chamber of Commerce can be very helpful in finding dog-friendly accommodations as well. Chambers of Commerce can usually provide a list of hotels and motels that accept dogs, and they may also be able to provide a list of local veterinarians. Vet's offices are usually aware of which local accommodations accept dogs.

Plan Family Vacations for the Whole Family

Your Boxer is just as much a part of the family as you and the kids. So why shouldn't she share in the fun you will be having on your next vacation? You've done your job well and your Boxer is well trained and well socialized. So why not reap some of the rewards of all your effort and have this well-behaved family member come along with you?

Granted, you may not find New York's Fifth Avenue or the Champs Élysées in Paris entirely appropriate for your Boxer, but all kinds of vacation plans can easily accommodate you and your pal. Besides, traveling with a dog has great rewards. You're more likely to meet new people in your travels if you have a dog with you. And if you're trying to keep the not-so-nice or downright dangerous people away, a Boxer is a great deterrent to those with less than honorable intentions. You can always feel confident that you are relatively safe with your Boxer standing by.

Lakeside cottages and mountain cabins provide a degree of privacy yet plenty of opportunity for family fun and social events in nearby towns. A good friend of mine spends a couple of weeks each year on a houseboat with his wife, daughter, and the family pooch. A hiking/camping trip provides lots of fun and adventure as well, not to mention giving you and your Boxer excellent exercise in the great outdoors.

Know What to Expect When You and Your Boxer Fly

If your plans include traveling by air, the whole picture becomes a bit more complicated. Air travel is not impossible, of course, but it's certainly not as easy as having your Boxer safely secured in the back of your family station wagon. Boxers won't exactly fit under the seat in front of you on an airplane, which means that you don't have the option of carrying your dog onboard. If your Boxer is going to travel with you by air, he must fly as excess baggage in the cargo hold of the plane at a cost of about $50 to $75 each way.

Air travel for dogs is no longer a unique situation. Hundreds of dogs accompany their owners back and forth across the country every day. The U.S. Department of Agriculture estimates that approximately 600,000 animals travel by air every year. A good percentage of that number is made up of dogs and cats. And the Air Transport Association reports that 99 percent of all animals shipped in the United States reach their destination "without incident." Of course, that remaining 1 percent of reported "incidents" includes everything from minor complaints to death.

Dogs travel in the cargo area of the plane, so even though this area is pressurized, there is no air-conditioning or heat control. Because of this, federal regulations require that no animal be shipped by air if the ground temperature at either end of the flight is above 85 degrees or below 45 degrees.

Air travel for pets is not entirely risk-free. But whenever travel by air is necessary, you can observe some safety measures that will help increase the odds of a safe arrival for your Boxer:

✔ **Check out the airlines.** Call the airlines you prefer and check out their policies regarding shipping dogs. Select the airline that offers the greatest safety assurances.

✔ **Make sure you understand the rules.** Airlines in general have all kinds of rules and regulations about what kind of crate they'll accept, how the crate should be identified, and where delivery and pickup must take place. In addition, individual airlines also enforce their own rules. Make sure you understand exactly what rules you must follow, well in advance of your departure date.

✔ **Make an advance reservation.** Most airlines will only accept a given number of dogs per flight. Reconfirm your flight, letting the airline know you're traveling with your dog, several times before the day of your flight.

✔ **Schedule a direct, nonstop flight.** Making connections, changing planes, and going through long stopovers are just some of the ways you increase the risk of loss and fatalities. Overnight and very early morning flights are the least crowded and offer better temperatures for your pet.

✔ **Talk with your vet before your trip.** Many states require a health certificate signed by a veterinarian, and nearly all airlines require one whether the state you're traveling to requires one or not. Discuss your travel plans with your vet. She may advise against shipping geriatric dogs, pregnant females, or any puppy less than eight weeks old. Always take your vet's advice! If she gives you the okay, discuss the need for tranquilizing your dog before shipping. But when it comes to sedatives, avoid them if you can.

✔ **Give your dog a last-minute potty break.** Exercise your Boxer at the very last minute to make sure he has relieved himself.

✔ **Use an airline-approved shipping crate.** The crate you ship your dog in must be airline approved. If you don't want to take any chances, you can purchase one directly from the airline. The crate must be large enough for your dog to stand up and turn around in. This does not mean the crate should be the size of the Taj Mahal, however. If your dog has too much room, he could be jostled about during the flight.

✔ **Prepare the crate well.** Federal law requires absorbent bedding on the bottom of the crate. You must also supply food and water in dishes that are attached to the inside of the crate's wire door. Fill one of the shipping crate's water bowls and put it in your freezer the night before you ship your Boxer. Just before you leave home, take the frozen water out of the freezer and place it in the bowl in the crate. The ice will melt gradually and provide water for your Boxer for a longer period of time and with less spillage. Tape a small bag of food to the top of the crate along with food and water instructions for the next 24 hours in case of delays. You are not allowed to put a lock on the crate door; however, you can offer double security with bungee cords or tape.

✔ **Mark the crate.** You must include a "live animal" sticker on the crate. These stickers are available from the airlines at your point of departure. Tape a sign on the crate, giving full information regarding contact persons at the point of departure and at your destination, with phone numbers and addresses.

✔ **Make sure your dog has a collar and ID tags.** Regardless of how careful the airline is, accidents do happen and a dog can manage to escape from her crate. If your Boxer eludes officials and gets beyond the airport premises, anyone who finds your dog won't have a way to contact you unless the dog carries identification. Include a telephone number on the tag at which someone can be reached 24 hours a day.

I've heard stories about owners who opened the crate at arrival only to have their dog bolt out in a panic without realizing the owner was even there. When you do arrive at your destination, your Boxer will be ecstatic to see you again after all those hours apart. But leave your dog in the crate until you get to a place that is less frantic and a bit safer than the airline terminal. Have a good sturdy leash with you in your carryon bag and snap the leash onto your dog while your pal is still in the crate.

Do not leave the leash on your Boxer when he is crated and in transit. The end of the leash could fall out of the crate and get caught on the conveyor belts that move cargo and luggage, which in turn could injure or kill your dog.

✔ **Arrive at the airport early.** Make it a practice to get to the airport a minimum of an hour and a half before flight time and go directly to the passenger check-in counter. Make sure the dog is fully checked in but insist that you stay where you can see the dog until the crate must be transported to the loading area. At that point, make a headlong dash for the gate and watch to see that your dog is loaded on the plane. When you get on board, have the attendant check to make sure the dog actually is on board. Will this make you seem like a bit of a nuisance? Perhaps. But it's better than arriving at your destination only to find your Boxer is somewhere else.

Find a Good Kennel for Your Boxer if He Can't Come with You

Although it may be great fun to have your Boxer along, it just may not be practical. What then? Cancel the trip? Well, you could. Or, as an alternative, you could find a good boarding kennel to take care of your pal while you're gone.

Drop by the kennels you're considering and ask if you can have a tour. Are food and water containers kept clean? Do the runs show signs of regular care and cleaning? Look at what the surface of the runs is made of. Do they provide good footing and easy cleanup and sanitizing? Is the run your dog will be kept in of sufficient size? If not, what provisions are made for exercise? What about security? Are the runs escape-proof?

Even though your practically perfect Boxer may not be a fighter, the dog in the next run at a boarding kennel just may be and could encourage your paci-fist to do battle. Look at the fencing and make sure it provides safety without making the dog feel totally cut off from the world.

Discuss your dog's attitude toward strangers and ask the kennel manager and employees what their views of Boxers are. If your Boxer wants and needs attention, make sure the kennel attendants will be able to provide this. Many kennels provide what they call *play time,* when your dog has time in a large paddock and someone to play catch with. They may charge a few dollars per day for this service, but it can mean a big difference in your pal's stay.

Ask the manager what inoculations and health precautions boarders are required to have when they check in. Are incoming dogs screened for fleas, ticks, and other parasites? If there are no requirements regarding health safe-guards, look elsewhere.

When you check your pal in be sure to leave your veterinarian's name, address, and phone number in case of emergency. And also leave a contact number where you can be reached while you're away. Take your Boxer's blan-ket or bed and plenty of her favorite toys. Bring enough food for your Boxer to last for the duration of your absence.

Consider the Advantage of Pet Sitters

A pet sitter is someone who will come to your home at regular intervals during the day to feed and provide time for your dog to exercise and take care of those calls of nature. Although you won't be home to hold your Boxer's paw, with a pet sitter everything else remains the same. If your Boxer isn't happier about this, at least *you* will be.

If you're only going to be away for a couple days, you can probably find a friend or relative who gets along well with your Boxer and who won't mind coming over to feed him and let him out. But if your absence is going to extend beyond a couple days, consider paying someone to come in to take care of your dog. Your vet may be able to recommend someone. National organizations dedicated to making recommendations for qualified pet sitters are a great help, too.

Contact the National Association of Professional Pet Sitters, 1030 15th Street NW, Suite 870, Washington, DC 20005 (telephone: 800-296-7387; Web site: www.petsitters.org) or Pet Sitters International, 418 East King Street, King, NC 27021 (telephone: 800-268-7487; Web site: www.petsit.com) for referrals.

Most professional pet sitters provide credentials and written agreements as to what they will and will not do and what they agree to be responsible for. Find a sitter who knows and understands the Boxer and whom your Boxer will get along with. A professional pet sitter who is a member of a national pet-sitting organization is usually bonded and insured. Any dog lover can advertise himself as a "professional," but be sure your pet sitter is bonded and insured for your own protection. You don't want to come home to find your Boxer is sitting there waiting for you in a home stripped of every valuable you have accumulated in a lifetime.

Chapter 16

Ten Ways to Have Fun with Your Boxer

In This Chapter

▶ Knowing which games a Boxer plays naturally

▶ Finding dog-friendly parks

▶ Participating in water sports with your Boxer

▶ Keeping in mind ecology when you and your Boxer are at play

▶ Playing fun sports with rules

*B*oxers are nothing if not playful. And as a dog owner, you can play with your Boxer in organized activities or on your own in your own backyard. In this chapter, I give you ten great suggestions for ways to have fun with your new best friend.

Play with a Bouncing Ball

Balls and Boxers go together. Old, beat up footballs, basketballs, and soccer balls can usually be picked up at garage sales and flea markets for next to nothing. And they can provide more fun for your Boxer, your kids, and yourself than the most expensive dog toy the pet stores could possibly offer.

Kick that soccer ball around while your Boxer plays guard, and the two of you could go on for hours. A good many Boxers become so expert at guarding the ball that their human opponents have to be on their toes to even *think* of getting past them. Basketballs are too big for Boxers to grasp, so they very quickly learn to manipulate the ball with their noses.

A Boxer can become so engrossed in nudging the ball back and forth that she can forget about time or possible danger. So make sure you only allow your Boxer to play ball on her own in a safe area. Your own fenced yard is fine (if the posies don't mind being trampled on!). Never allow your Boxer to play ball in an area where there is danger of traffic. Chasing the ball will be far more important to your dog than watching for careless drivers.

When you're selecting a ball for a puppy, make sure the ball is larger than what the puppy can fit into his mouth and attempt to swallow. If the ball fits inside the puppy's mouth, it could easily get lodged in the dog's throat and cause the puppy to choke.

Get Your Dog to Fetch

Some Boxers love to fetch things you've thrown, and they'll play this game by the hour. Others look at you like, "Well, she mustn't want it if she threw it away." Most Boxer puppies will chase after just about anything that rolls along or flies through the air. Getting the pup to bring it back to you may prove to be a different story. The easiest way to get around that is to start off with two balls or toss toys. Throw one a few feet away. When the puppy picks it up, he may do a lot of proud prancing and dancing around. Encourage the pup to come back by offering lots of praise and waving the second toy. Getting the pup interested in the second toy will bring the youngster back to you, and if you indicate you are going to throw it again, the pup will probably drop the first toy or ball in front of you. When the pup does drop the toy, give lots of praise.

The pup will soon get the idea that you will not be throwing again until the object is brought back to you. When the puppy returns with the object but does not want to relinquish his hold, you can gently remove the toy from the dog's mouth and say "drop," as you place the toy on the ground.

Play Hide-and-Seek

Hide-and-seek is a game that can be played two different ways. First, you can be the hider. This works best when you have someone to hold your Boxer's leash while you find a nearby place to hide. Call the dog's name and have the other person unsnap the leash and say, "Find!" Keep calling until the dog finds you, and then give lots of praise. Eventually you won't have to call out and the person holding the dog will only have to say "Find."

Another variation of hide-and-seek is done with one of your dog's favorite toys like a ball or a Kong. Rub the toy briskly between the palms of your hands. Let your dog see the toy, but then have the holder distract the dog while you go off and conceal the object in a place that is, at first, close by.

Have the holder release and give the *find* command. You can stand near the hidden object and also repeat the *find* command. If the toy is one that the dog knows by name, use a command like "find the squeaky" or "find the ball." You may have to lead the dog to the toy a time or two, but most Boxers get the idea very quickly. When your Boxer gets the idea, you won't have to stand near the object at all.

If you don't have anyone to help you with these hide-and-seek games, you can give your Boxer the *sit and stay* command while you hide the toy or yourself out of the dog's sight. When you've hidden the toy (or yourself), give the *okay* command to let your dog know it is okay to get up. Then follow the *okay* with *find*.

Visit a Dog-Friendly Park

Unfortunately, because of neglectful dog owners finding parks and recreational areas that allow dogs or that permit dogs to be off leash is becoming increasingly difficult. Not all people love dogs as much as you and I. Even those who like dogs don't appreciate being harassed or threatened by someone else's dog. Although your well-trained Boxer would never think to threaten anyone, many people are thoroughly convinced that all Boxers are dangerous and become terrified at the sight of one, particularly if the dog is off leash.

Keep your Boxer on a leash at all times when you are in a public recreation area. The retractable leashes that extend up to 25 feet work great. If no one else is around to bother you, you can extend your dog the full distance. But you can also have constant control over your dog at all times and retract the leash when people are around.

If you want to use a nearby park, check with your local Department of Parks and Recreation to see what kinds of rules exist regarding dogs. Some parks allow dogs only during certain hours, when there is less public use. Some parks even allow dogs to be off leash during specified time periods.

Many communities are creating special *dog parks* or fencing in certain portions of public parks to allow dogs to be off leash. The value of these dedicated areas is that they give your dog plenty of opportunity for some serious exercise by running with other canine pals and help improve socialization. But when you're trying out an off-leash dog park, remember that you and your dog are the new kids on the block. Proceed with care and make sure there are no bullies present. If one dog seems determined to rule the pack through aggression, take your Boxer home and try the park at another time.

Have Fun in the Water

Some Boxers love water; others hate it. But you can pretty much guarantee that your Boxer will hate the water forever if you throw him into the water on his first visit to the beach. Allow the dog to become accustomed to the water gradually, and nine times out of ten you'll wind up with an excellent swimmer on your hands.

I usually take a puppy who hasn't been introduced to the ocean down to the beach on a calm day when the surf is relatively gentle. The sound and ominous look of huge crashing waves can be very frightening to a pup. Try to bring along an older dog who likes the water. This gives the pup or new dog confidence that he will not be eaten alive by this huge wet beast.

If you don't have a seasoned dog for your dog to follow, attach a long leash to your dog's collar and walk at a leisurely pace, allowing your dog to trail along and very gradually get his feet wet. If you walk too rapidly, the pup will begin to splash himself — and cold water on the tummy can be a little intimidating for the first-timer.

When your Boxer does decide that water sports are the next best thing to a steak dinner, be sure the dog doesn't become totally exhausted. Some dogs will retrieve sticks or balls out of the water for as long as there is someone around to throw for them. But you don't want your dog to get tired and unable to swim back to shore.

Ocean and river swimming can be dangerous because of currents, riptides, and the size of the surf. If you wouldn't let your child swim where you are, don't allow your Boxer to do so. Talk to lifeguards or people familiar with the beaches and tides in your area so that you don't make the fatal mistake of sending your Boxer off into a hazardous situation.

Figure 16-1:
Boxers and kids love the water — and each other. Just be sure to watch both of them and keep them safe.

Photograph courtesy of Richard Tomita

Responsible beach-going

Ocean and lake ecology is at an extremely fragile state, and most conservationists would like to keep dogs off of our beaches entirely. Today's commercial dog foods contain many additives that are not environmentally friendly. When dogs eliminate along beaches, the harmful materials contained in their food eventually wash down into the waters and are capable of killing off marine life.

You may think that your dog depositing his feces on the beach once a day or once a week could not possibly do any great harm to vast bodies of water. But multiply what your dog is responsible for by the hundreds of dogs who live in your area and the number of days and weeks in a year and you can see where the problem lies. If you take your Boxer to the beach, plan to pick up any droppings. Commercial concerns do enough damage to our waters. We who profess to be nature lovers and lovers of all animals shouldn't be contributing to the problem.

When you are on the beach, keep your dog on a leash unless you are in an entirely remote area where it is practical and legal for the dog to run free. Keep in mind the fact that many people go to the beach to relax and read and do not include having someone's massive Boxer leaping over them or kicking sand in their face as part of the plan.

Swimming pools have no tides or surf to contend with, but make sure your Boxer is completely familiar with how and where to get out. Begin by taking your dog down to the far end of the pool and then allow the dog to follow you and exit in the way that will be easiest for the dog to use, by walking up the stairs for example. Do this several times and your Boxer will quickly learn how to get out on her own. Never leave a dog in or near a pool unless you are absolutely certain that the dog is able to get out of the pool alone. And your dog is never completely safe unless you're nearby to intervene in case of an emergency.

Hike the Trails with Your Dog

Hiking on the beautiful trails cut through some of our national parks is a wonderful experience. And who better to share the beauty of it with than your Boxer pal? Your dog may not relate to it on the aesthetic level that you do, but rest assured that she's able to enjoy her sniffs and discoveries of the day as much as you do in your way. The camaraderie and the invigorating exercise make for a perfect dog owner's day.

Be sure to bring the proper equipment with you on your hikes. Stash in your backpack any emergency and first aid materials that may be appropriate to the time of the year and the terrain. Park rangers and the Department of Parks and Recreation can advise you on what you should carry in case of emergency.

Hiking supplies for both dog and dog owner are available at specialty shops and through catalogs. In fact, hiking with dogs has become so popular that a wide range of equipment is geared to the canine set alone: collapsible food and drink containers, booties to protect your dog's feet from sharp rocks or freezing terrain, rainwear, even doggie sun shades and sun glasses. And just so all of your Boxer's camping and hiking equipment doesn't become an additional burden for you, there are doggie backpacks designed to help your dog carry whatever she needs along the trail.

Most national parks allow dogs but have very strict leash laws to protect the wildlife. Dog have trouble resisting the chase, especially when a rabbit or deer is the one they get to follow. And because most urban dogs are not trained for the woods, their chase can lead them miles away before they realize they are lost.

Dog lover or not, no one wants to step in dog droppings along the trail. Carry your own disposable baggies to pick up your dog's waste and a larger plastic bag to carry the matter in until you come upon the proper place to deposit trash.

Try Flyball with Your Boxer

In *flyball,* dogs are organized into four teams. Each team races on a relay system. At the signal, each dog must clear four hurdles, release a ball from the flyball box, catch it in the air, and return with the ball to the starting point so that the next dog on the team can start off. The team is racing against the clock. And the speed and excitement make for a very enthusiastic ringside.

Flyball is certainly one of the most exciting activities you and your Boxer can do together. The degree to which your Boxer is obsessed with his tennis balls may help you determine to some degree how successful he may be as a participant in this event.

Three titles can be earned in the sport: Flyball Dog (FD), Flyball Dog Excellent (FDX), and Flyball Dog Champion (FDCh). You can get information regarding rules, training, and where events are held directly from the North American Flyball Association, Inc. (NAFA). The association can be contacted at its main headquarters: 1400 West Devon Avenue #512, Chicago, IL 60660; telephone: 309-688-9840; Web site: www.flyball.org.

Playing the Sport of Freestyle

Freestyle is a relatively new canine sport, with one paw in obedience and the other in dance and/or calisthenics. Many of the basic obedience exercises are called upon in the sport, but freestyle requires many more movements from the dog, all in a routine set to music.

In the United States, there are two main approaches to freestyle. The Canine Freestyle Federation (CFF) puts the spotlight primarily on the dogs and their movements, with the handlers being as inconspicuous as possible. The other approach, governed by the Musical Canine Sports International (MCSI), is a bit more flamboyant, with more emphasis on the handler's costuming and movement. Both approaches seem to attract staunch followers, and both are growing rapidly in popularity.

Teamwork and coordination are prime factors in this event. Scoring is based upon the performance of both the dog and the handler. Execution of some of the standard obedience movements is required but nonstandard movements that the dogs are called upon to perform also weigh heavily. Enthusiasm, degree of difficulty of the movements displayed, and appropriateness of music and its interpretation are additional scoring factors. Both organizations are able to provide in-depth discussions of their respective approaches and membership in each or both organizations can be obtained on the Internet. Check out the Canine Freestyle Federation at `www.canine-freestyle.org` or write them directly c/o Monica Patty, Corresponding Secretary, 21900 Foxden Lane, Leesburg, VA 20175. The organization's telephone number is 703-327-4860. Musical Canine Sports International can be contacted at its Canadian Headquarters by writing them c/o Val Culpin, 3466 Creston Drive, Abbotsford, British Columbia, Canada V2T 5B9.

Take Frisbee to the Next Level

Not all dogs are mad about playing Frisbee. But if your Boxer decides that catching that plastic disc while it flies through the air is a jolly good time, it could well become an obsession. Some Boxers take to catching and retrieving a Frisbee at their first try and get better and better with each catch. Other Boxers need to develop a liking for the object first, and one of the easiest ways to do this is to initially use the Frisbee as a food dish.

Whether your Boxer's interest is mild or extreme, playing Frisbee is excellent exercise and can help keep your pal in great shape. If you find your Boxer is a Frisbee fanatic, there's no limit to the heights to which the two of you can soar.

If Frisbee seems like something you and your canine athlete may be interested in, countless books, Web sites, and videos can help launch you and your dog on your way to stardom.

Local, regional, national, and international Frisbee competitions are held year-round. And prizes range anywhere from a couple of hundred dollars into the thousands. There are even international Frisbee teams that meet annually for the World Cup of Frisbee!

Take Part in Agility Competition

Agility competition is essentially an obstacle course for dogs. Everyone involved (and everyone who watches) appears to be having the time of their lives. The sport has become outrageously popular at dog shows and fairs throughout the world. The canine contestants have to maneuver their way (off leash) through tunnels, cat walks, seesaws, and numerous other obstacles — and they're timed in the process.

Agility competition started in England and caught the public's attention when it was first presented at the world-famed Crufts Dog Show in London in 1978. By 1986 it was already a major event in Great Britain and had caught on so well in the United States that the United States Dog Agility Association (USDAA) was organized.

The enthusiasm of the dogs and the supportive roar of the ringside as their favorite dog jumps over, under, around, and through the obstacles gives an electric feeling to the event. And the canine participants seem to thrive on it all. Agility competition does take teamwork, because the handler has to act as navigator. Although the dogs do all the maneuvering, the handler is the one who directs the dog where to go, because the sequence of the individual obstacles is different at every event.

Both the American Kennel Club and the U.S. Dog Agility Association, Inc., can provide additional information as well as names and addresses of the organizations sponsoring events nearest to your home. Contact the USDAA through its Web site at www.usdaa.com or by telephone at 972-231-9700. You can write the USDAA at P.O. Box 850955, Richardson, TX 75085-0955. The AKC (5580 Centerview Drive, Raleigh, NC 27606), also provides information on its Agility programs at its Web site, www.akc.org, or by telephone at 919-233-3627.

Appendix A

Glossary

Agility Excellent (AX): A title awarded to dogs who qualify the required number of times in the Agility Excellent class at AKC Agility Trials.

albino: A rare, genetically recessive condition characterized by white hair and pink eyes.

American Kennel Club (AKC): Organization that registers purebred dogs and sanctions dog shows and other competitions.

angulation: The angles formed by the meeting of the dog's bones; usually in respect to the bones of the forequarters and hindquarters.

balanced: A term used to signify that a dog is a symmetrically and proportionally correct.

Best in Show (BIS): Designation for the best dog at an all-breed show.

Best in Specialty Show (BISS): Designation for the best dog at a Boxer-only show.

Best of Breed (BOB): Designation for the best Boxer at an all-breed show.

Best of Winners (BOW): Winners Dog (WD) and Winners Bitch (WB) compete to see which is the best of the two. The winner is given this award.

Best Opposite Sex (BOS): After Best of Breed (BOB) is awarded, the best individual of the opposite sex receives this award.

bitch: A female dog.

Bitter Apple: A liquid used to discourage dogs from licking or chewing on themselves or household objects.

body language: A dog's method of communicating his reactions.

brindle: A color pattern resulting in the layering of black markings over regions of lighter color (in Boxers, over tan) producing somewhat of a tiger-striped pattern.

Canine Eye Registration Foundation (CERF): Organization that tests and certifies eyes against genetic diseases.

Canine Good Citizen: Basic test of a dog's good manners and stability. Passing the test earns an official CGC designation, which can be added to the successful dog's name.

castration: Surgical removal of the testicles of the male dog. Also known as *neutering.*

Champion (CH): Winner of 15 American Kennel Club (AKC) championship points under three different judges. Two of the wins must be *majors* (with three or more points).

character: The general appearance and/or expression that is considered typical of the breed.

Companion Dog (CD): Official initial Obedience degree, which can be earned by competing in the Obedience Novice class. Comparable to a person's high school diploma.

Companion Dog Excellent (CDX): Next up from the initial Companion Dog Obedience degree. Comparable to a person's college degree.

condition: A dog's overall appearance of health or lack thereof.

conformation: The form and structure of a dog as required by the respective breed standard of perfection.

cryptorchid: Male dog whose testicles are not visible.

dentition: Arrangement of the teeth.

down: The command used to instruct a dog to lie down.

estrus: Season or heat that is part of the female reproductive cycle during which ovulation occurs.

fawn: A brown color influenced by red/yellow that can range from light tan to dark mahogany.

Federacion Cynologique Internationale (FCI): Controlling body of pedigreed dogs in most European and Latin American countries.

gait: Manner in which the pattern of footsteps varies at different rates of speed.

Group First-Fourth: Indicates a dog has earned a placement in Variety Group competition at an all-breed show.

heartworm: A parasitic worm that invades the heart and lungs of a dog and can so affect those organs as to become fatal. Veterinary medication is required.

heel: The command given to a dog so that he will walk along at the handler's left side with his shoulder in line with the handler's knee.

hip dysplasia (HD): Abnormal development of the hip affecting the dog in varying degrees of intensity.

hookworm: An internal parasite that can create an anemic condition.

incisors: The teeth located between the fangs in the front of the upper and lower jaw.

International Championship (Int.Ch.): A degree that can only be awarded by the Federacion Cynologique Internationale (FCI).

level bite: A bite in which the front or incisor teeth meet exactly, top to bottom.

Lyme disease: A disease transported by ticks; can create joint and neurological problems in both dogs and humans.

molars: Rear teeth; used for chewing.

monorchid: A male dog who has only one apparent testicle.

neutering: Surgical removal of the testicles of the male dog. Also known as *castration.*

oestrus: Stage of the reproductive cycle in which the female will stand willing for mating.

Orthopedic Foundation for Animals (OFA): An organization that certifies x-rays of hips and elbows.

overshot: A bite in which the front or incisor teeth of the top jaw overlap the front or incisor teeth of the lower jaw.

parent club: The national club of a breed. The American Boxer Club is the parent club for Boxers in the United States.

Schutzhund: German dog sport that tests a dog's excellence in obedience, protection, and tracking.

scissors bite: A bite in which the front upper teeth or incisors just barely overlap the lower front or incisor teeth of the lower jaw.

Sieger: Title awarded to the Best Male in a German *Sieger* show.

Siegerin: Title awarded to the Best Female in a German *Sieger* show.

sound: Overall good construction and health of a dog.

spaying: Surgically removing the ovaries of the female dog.

specialty show: A show restricted to only one breed of dog.

stay: Command given to a dog that requires remaining in one place until a release command is given.

stop: The step up from the muzzle to the skull; indentation between the eyes where the nasal bones and cranium meet.

SV: The largest and most influential breed organization in the world, of which Schutzhund training is an integral part.

therapy dogs: Dogs so trained as to bring comfort and companionship to hospitalized and elderly people.

tracking: Trials that test a dog's ability to track humans or lost articles.

type: The distinguishing characteristics of a breed as called for in the standard of the respective breed.

undershot: The front or incisor teeth of the lower jaw extend beyond the front or incisor teeth of the upper jaw.

Utility Dog: Advanced Obedience trial degree comparable to a person's graduate degree.

withers: The top of the first dorsal vertebra or highest part of the body just behind the neck. Often referred to as the top of the shoulders.

Working Dogs: A classification of dogs that includes breeds used to pull carts or sleds, to guard property, or to work in search and rescue operations.

Appendix B

Resources

● ●

*I*f you're looking for additional information on Boxers or on any of the concepts I cover in this book, consult one or more of the many wonderful
resources listed below.

Books

The Boxer, by Daniel Morris Gordon (published by Judy Publishing
Company, 1953)

The Boxer, by John P. Wagner (published by Orange Judd Publishing
Company, 1951)

Boxers: An Owner's Companion, by Ivor Ward-Davies (published by The
Crowood Press, 1991)

The Boxer: Family Favorite, by Stephanie Abraham (published by IDG Books
Worldwide, Inc.)

The Complete Boxer, by Tim Hutchings (published by IDG Books Worldwide,
Inc., 1998)

Complete Puppy and Dog Book, by Norman H. Johnson (published by Galahad
Books, 2000)

Dr. Pitcairn's Complete Guide to Natural Health for Dogs and Cats, by Richard
H. Pitcairn, D.V.M, Ph.D., and Susan Hubble Pitcairn (published by Rodale
Press, 1995)

How to Be Your Dog's Best Friend: A Training Manual for Dog Owners, by The
Monks of New Skete (published by Little, Brown and Company, 1978)

My Life with Boxers, by Friederun Stockmann, translated from the German by
Eric Fitch Daglish (published by Coward-McCann, 1968)

A New Owner's Guide to Boxers, by Richard Tomita (TFH Publications, 1996)

Schutzhund: Theory and Training Methods, by Susan Barwig and Stewart Hilliard (published by IDG Books Worldwide, Inc., 1991)

Superdog: Raising the Perfect Canine Companion, by Dr. Michael W. Fox (published by IDG Books Worldwide, Inc., 1990)

The World of the Boxer, by Richard Tomita (published by TFH Publications, 1998)

Magazines

Boxer Quarterly
Manor Farm Cottage, Lenton
Grantham, Lincs NG33 4HG
England

Boxer Review
8760 Appian Way
Los Angeles, California 90046
United States of America

Journal of Veterinary Medical Education
Dr. Richard B. Talbot, Editor
VA-MD College of Veterinary Medicine
Virginia Polytechnic Institute and State University
Blacksburg, Virginia 24061
United States of America
Web site: `scholar.lib.vt.edu/ejournals/JVME/V21-1/tofc.html`

Videos

The Boxer, American Kennel Club (Visit `www.akc.org/insideAKC/resources/vidbreed.cfm` for more information on this video, or call 919-233-3627 to order.)

Dog Steps, Rachel Page Elliot, American Kennel Club (Visit `www.akc.org/insideAKC/resources/vidbreed.cfm` for more information on this video, or call 919-233-3627 to order.)

Competitive Agility Training, Canine Training Systems (Visit `www.cts.productions.com` for more information on this video, or call 303-973-2107 to order.)

Web Sites

American Kennel Club: www.akc.org

American Boxer Club: clubs.akc.org/abc/abc-home.htm

Boxer Underground: www.boxerunderground.com

National Animal Poison Control Center: www.napcc.aspca.org

Organizations

American Boxer Club
Barbara E. Wagner, Corresponding Secretary
6310 Edward Drive
Clinton, Maryland 20735-4135

American Kennel Club
5580 Centerview Drive
Raleigh, North Carolina 27606-9767

United Kennel Club
100 East Kilgore Road
Kalamazoo, Michigan 49001

Index

F

G

• I •

• J •

• K •

• L •

• *U* •

Notes

Notes

Notes

Notes

Notes

Notes

Notes

Notes

Notes

Notes

Notes

Notes

FOR DUMMIES

The easy way to get more done and have more fun

PERSONAL FINANCE

0-7645-5231-7

0-7645-2431-3

0-7645-5331-3

Also available:

Estate Planning For Dummies
(0-7645-5501-4)

401(k)s For Dummies
(0-7645-5468-9)

Frugal Living For Dummies
(0-7645-5403-4)

Microsoft Money "X" For Dummies
(0-7645-1689-2)

Mutual Funds For Dummies
(0-7645-5329-1)

Personal Bankruptcy For Dummies
(0-7645-5498-0)

Quicken "X" For Dummies
(0-7645-1666-3)

Stock Investing For Dummies
(0-7645-5411-5)

Taxes For Dummies 2003
(0-7645-5475-1)

BUSINESS & CAREERS

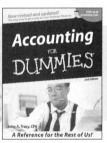

0-7645-5314-3

0-7645-5307-0

0-7645-5471-9

Also available:

Business Plans Kit For Dummies
(0-7645-5365-8)

Consulting For Dummies
(0-7645-5034-9)

Cool Careers For Dummies
(0-7645-5345-3)

Human Resources Kit For Dummies
(0-7645-5131-0)

Managing For Dummies
(1-5688-4858-7)

QuickBooks All-in-One Desk Reference For Dummies
(0-7645-1963-8)

Selling For Dummies
(0-7645-5363-1)

Small Business Kit For Dummies
(0-7645-5093-4)

Starting an eBay Business For Dummies
(0-7645-1547-0)

HEALTH, SPORTS & FITNESS

0-7645-5167-1

0-7645-5146-9

0-7645-5154-X

Also available:

Controlling Cholesterol For Dummies
(0-7645-5440-9)

Dieting For Dummies
(0-7645-5126-4)

High Blood Pressure For Dummies
(0-7645-5424-7)

Martial Arts For Dummies
(0-7645-5358-5)

Menopause For Dummies
(0-7645-5458-1)

Nutrition For Dummies
(0-7645-5180-9)

Power Yoga For Dummies
(0-7645-5342-9)

Thyroid For Dummies
(0-7645-5385-2)

Weight Training For Dummies
(0-7645-5168-X)

Yoga For Dummies
(0-7645-5117-5)

Available wherever books are sold.
Go to www.dummies.com or call 1-877-762-2974 to order direct.

FOR DUMMIES®

A world of resources to help you grow

HOME, GARDEN & HOBBIES

Feng Shui

0-7645-5295-3

Gardening

0-7645-5130-2

Guitar

0-7645-5106-X

Also available:

Auto Repair For Dummies
(0-7645-5089-6)

Chess For Dummies
(0-7645-5003-9)

Home Maintenance For
Dummies
(0-7645-5215-5)

Organizing For Dummies
(0-7645-5300-3)

Piano For Dummies
(0-7645-5105-1)

Poker For Dummies
(0-7645-5232-5)

Quilting For Dummies
(0-7645-5118-3)

Rock Guitar For Dummies
(0-7645-5356-9)

Roses For Dummies
(0-7645-5202-3)

Sewing For Dummies
(0-7645-5137-X)

FOOD & WINE

Cooking

0-7645-5250-3

Cookies

0-7645-5390-9

Wine

0-7645-5114-0

Also available:

Bartending For Dummies
(0-7645-5051-9)

Chinese Cooking For
Dummies
(0-7645-5247-3)

Christmas Cooking For
Dummies
(0-7645-5407-7)

Diabetes Cookbook For
Dummies
(0-7645-5230-9)

Grilling For Dummies
(0-7645-5076-4)

Low-Fat Cooking For
Dummies
(0-7645-5035-7)

Slow Cookers For Dummies
(0-7645-5240-6)

TRAVEL

Italy

0-7645-5453-0

Hawaii

0-7645-5438-7

Las Vegas

0-7645-5448-4

Also available:

America's National Parks For
Dummies
(0-7645-6204-5)

Caribbean For Dummies
(0-7645-5445-X)

Cruise Vacations For
Dummies 2003
(0-7645-5459-X)

Europe For Dummies
(0-7645-5456-5)

Ireland For Dummies
(0-7645-6199-5)

France For Dummies
(0-7645-6292-4)

London For Dummies
(0-7645-5416-6)

Mexico's Beach Resorts For
Dummies
(0-7645-6262-2)

Paris For Dummies
(0-7645-5494-8)

RV Vacations For Dummies
(0-7645-5443-3)

Walt Disney World & Orland
For Dummies
(0-7645-5444-1)

Available wherever books are sold. Go to www.dummies.com or call 1-877-762-2974 to order direct.

FOR DUMMIES®

Helping you expand your horizons and realize your potential

INTERNET

0-7645-0894-6

0-7645-1659-0

0-7645-1642-6

Also available:

America Online 7.0 For Dummies
(0-7645-1624-8)

Genealogy Online For Dummies
(0-7645-0807-5)

The Internet All-in-One Desk Reference For Dummies
(0-7645-1659-0)

Internet Explorer 6 For Dummies
(0-7645-1344-3)

The Internet For Dummies Quick Reference
(0-7645-1645-0)

Internet Privacy For Dummies
(0-7645-0846-6)

Researching Online For Dummies
(0-7645-0546-7)

Starting an Online Business For Dummies
(0-7645-1655-8)

DIGITAL MEDIA

0-7645-1664-7

0-7645-1675-2

0-7645-0806-7

Also available:

CD and DVD Recording For Dummies
(0-7645-1627-2)

Digital Photography All-in-One Desk Reference For Dummies
(0-7645-1800-3)

Digital Photography For Dummies Quick Reference
(0-7645-0750-8)

Home Recording for Musicians For Dummies
(0-7645-1634-5)

MP3 For Dummies
(0-7645-0858-X)

Paint Shop Pro "X" For Dummies
(0-7645-2440-2)

Photo Retouching & Restoration For Dummies
(0-7645-1662-0)

Scanners For Dummies
(0-7645-0783-4)

GRAPHICS

0-7645-0817-2

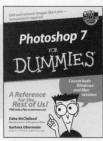

0-7645-1651-5

0-7645-0895-4

Also available:

Adobe Acrobat 5 PDF For Dummies
(0-7645-1652-3)

Fireworks 4 For Dummies
(0-7645-0804-0)

Illustrator 10 For Dummies
(0-7645-3636-2)

QuarkXPress 5 For Dummies
(0-7645-0643-9)

Visio 2000 For Dummies
(0-7645-0635-8)

FOR DUMMIES®

The advice and explanations you need to succeed

SELF-HELP, SPIRITUALITY & RELIGION

0-7645-5302-X

0-7645-5418-2

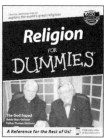
0-7645-5264-3

Also available:

The Bible For Dummies
(0-7645-5296-1)

Buddhism For Dummies
(0-7645-5359-3)

Christian Prayer For Dummies
(0-7645-5500-6)

Dating For Dummies
(0-7645-5072-1)

Judaism For Dummies
(0-7645-5299-6)

Potty Training For Dummies
(0-7645-5417-4)

Pregnancy For Dummies
(0-7645-5074-8)

Rekindling Romance For Dummies
(0-7645-5303-8)

Spirituality For Dummies
(0-7645-5298-8)

Weddings For Dummies
(0-7645-5055-1)

PETS

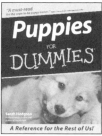
0-7645-5255-4

0-7645-5286-4

0-7645-5275-9

Also available:

Labrador Retrievers For Dummies
(0-7645-5281-3)

Aquariums For Dummies
(0-7645-5156-6)

Birds For Dummies
(0-7645-5139-6)

Dogs For Dummies
(0-7645-5274-0)

Ferrets For Dummies
(0-7645-5259-7)

German Shepherds For Dummies
(0-7645-5280-5)

Golden Retrievers For Dummies
(0-7645-5267-8)

Horses For Dummies
(0-7645-5138-8)

Jack Russell Terriers For Dummies
(0-7645-5268-6)

Puppies Raising & Training Diary For Dummies
(0-7645-0876-8)

EDUCATION & TEST PREPARATION

0-7645-5194-9

0-7645-5325-9

0-7645-5210-4

Also available:

Chemistry For Dummies
(0-7645-5430-1)

English Grammar For Dummies
(0-7645-5322-4)

French For Dummies
(0-7645-5193-0)

The GMAT For Dummies
(0-7645-5251-1)

Inglés Para Dummies
(0-7645-5427-1)

Italian For Dummies
(0-7645-5196-5)

Research Papers For Dummies
(0-7645-5426-3)

The SAT I For Dummies
(0-7645-5472-7)

U.S. History For Dummies
(0-7645-5249-X)

World History For Dummies
(0-7645-5242-2)

  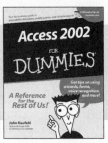

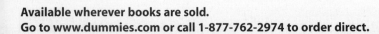